Wounded:

Fighting my demons

Vicky Hay

authorHOUSE®

AuthorHouse™ UK Ltd.
500 Avebury Boulevard
Central Milton Keynes, MK9 2BE
www.authorhouse.co.uk
Phone: 08001974150

First published by AuthorHouse 5/20/2010

ISBN: 978-1-4520-1905-5 (sc)

This book is printed on acid-free paper.

To Mike,

Thanks for everything so far,

Lots of lov Vicks x xxx.

In memory of Holly. The sparkling, pink angel in everyone's hearts.

iii

The birth of her

"She'll only live for two days if we do not intervene; we need to insert a naso gastric tube to reach her stomach to feed her. A glucose drip will go into her arm; she has collapsed and is weak. She refuses not only to eat, but to drink too, so yet another drip will be put up for fluids. We need to do an ECG to monitor her heart. She's frail but we are informed she WILL fight us."

I hear the words but am in disbelief: they're talking about me! Only a week before, I had the luxury of 'freedom': out with my friends, shopping and partying, yet there was little time for me to eat and drink. I felt invincible, that I could keep going, run on empty, and no-one or nothing could stop me.

I'm nineteen at this point. I have suffered in secret since I was about twelve, from the crippling disease that is anorexia, but about a year and a half ago they hung the label around my neck but even since then, my body continues to be punished.

At this stage I have already been in hospital three times, a process of feeding, talking, and feeding some more, but each time I'm allowed to return home, and back to what I now know best: anorexia.

The week before this conversation started I walked blindly

with false hope, to my weekly appointment with my consultant psychiatrist. I was on some sort of starvation high. My weight was falling faster than ever, yet I was embracing life like never before. I was convinced I was happy, a kind of euphoria that I believed would only continue with the more weight I lost. My body looked frail but my heart felt strong. I eventually believed I was one of my friends. I no longer felt like the insecure, outsider. I felt loved as I was accepting myself more.

I was confused on arrival to the appointment that we were not in my consultant's usual room. And not alone. I was soon to learn that this other person was a second opinion psychiatrist.

I sat and I'm sure I came across content as I lied about the food and water I had consumed during the week, but bones protruded through my loose clothes. Out of no-where my world fell apart. He used two words and I knew it was game over: "you're sectioned". This was under the mental health act. They believed I was a risk to myself. I was refusing to accept treatment, I did not see the need or have the want to change my well ingrained ways; my anorexic driven life-style. Mum says she knew it was coming, I was oblivious. I had heard of people being sectioned before but never believed it would happen to me. So there I was: prisoner to a place that would scare me like no other and the battle of a lifetime began.

Anorexia snuck up upon me and reared its head like the beast it is. In the beginning I felt blessed by her presence. I will refer to anorexia as 'her' throughout this book as this is how I picture it: this skeletal girl in my mind, pushing me to be more like her. I know her weight, the way she lives her life: mine had to mirror that exactly. Her frail model-like frame; seducing and louring me, a feeble hand placed on my too large shoulders, and guiding me to a place where she will no longer torment me. I feared ever losing her, losing control. She was what my whole life had become and I felt I needed her.

I've met girls whose anorexia has just suddenly crept up on them, and with this, taken over their minds and life's. I thought this was me too – but therapy was to show me differently.

Before I can tell you about the hospital admissions, tubes, thoughts, and fights, I need to give you a picture of my early life:

My childhood memories are generally very happy. Nothing traumatic or disturbing happened to make me feel a need to take some kind of drastic control or not accept who I was.

I was always an easily embarrassed child, and now adult. I hated doing things wrong or people pointing out my faults; my self-esteem could not take it. I am a perfectionist through and through, and wanted to always get everything right and to please everyone. Anorexia was soon to become my greatest strive for faultlessness.

I loved primary school: I was popular, carefree, and bright, I always had a younger mind than my age – but loved it. But despite this, it was here I began experimenting with dieting. I'm the youngest of three girls and with a considerable age gap I was open to a 'grown up' world that my young mind should maybe not have been subject to. I lived in a grown up house, was surrounded by adults, but my mind was most definitely a child's: it absorbed absolutely everything. My sisters were diet fanatics. They counted fat, and gave me books on calories. We even had a picture of a girl standing on a set of scales, plastered on our biscuit tin. What did that tell a nine year old?

I think I just believed that this was life. Everyone dieted and I should too. It wasn't until I was admitted to a hospital aged eighteen, that I realised that people did actually eat. I though everyone existed on salads and vegetables.

I am now also told that I come from a 'typically anorexic family'. I did not think there was such a thing, and it seems like such a horrible label to give us. The reasons are, however, that I have a dad who, though we lived together, wasn't the 'hands on' type. I remember wandering as a child if my dad even knew my friends names. He was, and still is a very hard worker, and it seemed that work was where his focus had to lie. Mum and dad used to fight a lot; I was left wandering, at a young age, if they actually loved each other. I have such respect for him as he provided me with everything I became accustomed to. I feel I am more like him than anyone may know, and suspect this is one of the reasons our bond is strained. Hating me meant disliking him.

My mum is the other extreme. She has always been very overprotective of me, grounding me by any means possible. She worries constantly about me and my sisters, but I guess maybe more so me, because I am the youngest. As I was not the most confident child, she felt the need to shelter me more. She always had, and has my very best interest at heart, but at times kept my feet too firmly on the ground, therefore decreasing my independence and ambitions for the future. I started to doubt I could do anything alone and thereafter became needy. My sister too suffered from anorexia as a child. I recall nothing of this, but it makes me wander, 'Why my family?'

I can recall comparing my leg width to girls in my class at the age of ten, always thinking I was so much bigger. Looking back I see I was generally the skinniest – the mind games of the future had begun. I'd test out 'healthy' eating diets but knew that not eating was the only way to really get thin. When others may have opted for an apple rather than crisps; I would choose neither.

I was an incredibly fussy child. Mum remembers going on holiday and having to take a cool box of food as I would refuse everything offered. I liked everything plain and hated trying new things. Therefore I was, at this early age, eating less than most others, and was already underweight. However I had the sweetest tooth: I could live without normal food, but sweets and chocolate were my weakness. Mum rarely stored these. These would be demons of my future. Primary seven, aged 11 was my last childhood memories of happiness. I loved my teacher, my friends and lifestyle…it was all soon to change!

Secondary school was where things took a turn for the worst. I was suddenly launched into a world of popularity, bitchiness, and rejection. I no longer felt the peace and freedom I did as a child. You had to grow up; it was a battle of the best.

I hung around with the 'cool' kids to start with but it soon became apparent that some of us were not welcome; we did not fit the bill. It hurt, as rejection does, but when you're already a vulnerable kid with little confidence in yourself, you take it bad.

Don't get me wrong, I had a group of friends, but I had this deep seated feeling that we were the misfits. The popular group were all the same; all beautiful, similar sizes, and had a confidence I felt they deserved. None of my group were; we were all different shapes and sizes, had different interests and fashion senses. I'm ashamed to admit but I was embarrassed by us. I recall feeling so ugly. It made me so miserable. I believed that because I was the youngest of three and not planned, my sisters had got all the looks and I was left with all the bad parts. I felt envious and in desperate need for my life to pan out as theirs did. I saw the perfection in their lives and I wanted it for my own. I would express my distress to friends, but I guess it was just seen as part of growing up and did not scream out my low self-esteem and self-worth. My friends also hated the popular group, but I'm sure their distress did not lead to self-destruction.

I see now that I became quite depressed about the whole 'school' situation. I hated going and wished I could move schools to get away from the popular ones. I hated – despised, if I became the focus of their attention. Each word would cut as deep as the blades in the future. There was no escaping it at times. I see now they were just being kids, but I took everything too personally. Things they would forget about I still replay over in my mind today. I had a major passion for dancing, yet here too my self esteem took a beating. I wasn't 'perfect' compared to the others. I did not have the confidence to shine. Their skeletal bodies reeked havoc on my mind – I proved my ability but fifteen years too late!

My dieting soon started to take over. I think I was trying to make myself more attractive, thinking that the popular crowd would maybe accept me then. Every magazine expressed thinness as beauty: I believed every word. I remember suggesting to a friend that I just chew my food and spit it out to avoid the calories. She told her mum who was a nurse who said it could lead to an eating disorder, so I rejected it. Still I was oblivious to my minds power, as was everyone around me. I did not want an eating disorder, but was convinced my size eight body was fat.

It's strange but I have such clear memories of situations

where food was involved. I remember in first year my friends went to the chip shop for lunch. I bought chips but was terrified and felt it was the wrong thing to do. I was showered with guilt. My guilt was reinforced when I went home and my sister said if I ate chips I would get fat. The thought horrified me and was enough to put me off for life. I convinced myself, along with much other foods, I hated them. Also, I would allow myself 'treats', like biscuits or cakes, but only if it was a special occasion, like my birthday, no other time. My friends ridiculed me for it. I couldn't understand how they could allow themselves these things every day. On holiday in Florida I recall eating a low fat muffin every morning and being petrified that it would increase my weight. I was eleven. These feelings were too fuelled by opinions my family had on certain foods. My sisters were extremely diet and exercise focused, and I was sucked in.

I was soon eating nothing but my evening meal and fruit. I'd cut out breakfast after watching a film in home economics that said not eating breakfast would make you lose weight. This 'fact' clicked and there was no going back. I had cut out snacks as the school nurse had frowned upon me eating crisps every break time. I felt so ashamed and guilty as though she was calling me greedy and unhealthy. I was twelve! I can remember sitting in her room and wanting to tell her that I thought I was over-weight, yet knowing I really was not. I could not understand my mixed emotions.

Not eating made me tired and low. My friends expressed concern and my mind worked in over time. This was something new; I was getting attention for once in my life. I had found something and was clinging onto it. But more than I wanted the attention, I wanted to feel thin. A friend said to my guidance teacher that I wasn't eating enough, but I could talk myself out of any situation. I would explain in great detail to my mum what I had eaten at school each day: all lies. She would question why I no longer had an after school snack; I would tell her that I'd eaten sweets bought from the school van. She deemed this as BAD. I felt ashamed, even though it was all lies.

I obviously lost weight, but it was not really too noticeable as I was a changing teenager. I felt better. But dieting got harder at times. I would feel extreme guilt if I had a 'bad' eating day and beat myself up further. In my diary I had a symbol of an angel for days my diet was strict and minimal, and a devil for days when I felt I had been 'bad', by eating extra cereal or the odd sweet treat. I saw nothing wrong with this. Anorexia was burrowing deep, but she placed a blindfold over my innocent eyes.

I threw myself into school work. I became obsessed with studying, and I was so scared of failing anything – a perfectionist trait of many anorexics. I would study from the minute I got home until my head hit the pillow. I rejected friends, socialising, and any form of enjoyment. I studied, exercised and starved. This drew unwanted attention. I felt trapped. I guess this was part of my obsessive compulsive disorder (OCD) behaviour: where you feel constrained to do something in the fear if you do not, disaster will occur. I was compelled to do more than I needed. I felt if I did not do all the things I did, then bad things would happen to me. My OCD grew from there.

My family labelled me as 'moody' at home as they had no clue as to what was going on. I hated that characterisation - it hurt, and to this day I cannot stand being called it. It has such negative connotations. My sister Karen was always so bright and excitable; so loved. I felt like the reject. My jealousy about her manifested as I wanted to be like her so much. I wanted to feel the love she got. I had her placed on a pedestal. Even now I feel her life is perfect; with her gorgeous fiancé and two beautiful children. I believed that if I was her then my life would be so much better.

Even in the early stages I was quite competitive about dieting. I would try to deter my friends from it and if they did start, I would make my own rules harsher. I couldn't stand the thought of other people losing weight. I was scared they got thinner than me. I wanted it to be my thing. I felt it was all I had. I was so fearful of these obsessive feelings of fatness. It felt so uncomfortable. I felt like a dead weight and losing weight would make me 'lighter' in every sense. I wanted to look like the models; I believed they looked anorexic. I wanted to look like them and would constantly write so in my diary. I did not quite comprehend anorexia was a disease of the mind. As a teenager I was constantly at the doctors for sore throats, constipation, tiredness and my lack of periods, yet still no-one mentioned anorexia. But I do not blame the doctors as I was the one living it and even I was still oblivious.

6th year came at school and things took a turn for the better. People left and our classes were mixed, and I found I was becoming part of the group I had put so far above me for so long. We had a common room where we mixed and bonded. Shannon was who I especially found closeness with. I was more like them than I though and seemed to fit in well. They were not scary or intentionally hurtful, but my insecurities remained. I felt I had to be on my guard, watch what I said and act and think like them. These people became, and still are my best friends, and without them I do not know how I would cope. So here is the first of many thank you to them. I started part-time work in a restaurant as did they, and connected with Kirsty. But in later years I had to leave this job, unknown to others, because of my fear of the food. The summer I left school, twelve of us went on an all girls holiday to Malia. Blind to my illness I had the most astounding time. It is one of the few times I recall feeling truly happy. I ate very little. There was some voiced concern but I was content. Shanon and I became inseparable. Often I long to be that seventeen year old again: carefree, loving life and oblivious to the disease controlling her.

My eating however was too ingrained to change. I did not know there was a problem. I believed everyone had the dream to be thinner and I was just trying to fulfil mine. Little did I know that soon I would be engulfed in a dieting world of my own?

New Year new me?

JAN 1ST 2005: So it's the start of a new year, and I feel fat and disgusting, as always. Christmas seems the only time I let the diet slip. I starve in November but then overdo it with treats at Christmas. So January means business; diet, diet, diet and gym everyday! I know I have to get a body like Victoria and Nicole.

But the amount of exercise I was doing was firing up my appetite. I was finding it hard to eat nothing like I wanted to, so I'd eat and be wreaked with guilt. I hated it. I despised my body, and along with food it was all I ever thought about.

Towards the middle of the month I started to feel unwell, not the self-induced unwell I would soon feel, but more flu like symptoms. I visited my GP a couple of times and blood was taken. Late one night I got a call saying that the tests showed that I had glandular fever, my immune system was zero, and I must go straight to hospital. It was quite exciting in some strange way, people fussing in my midnight arrival to ward 43. I stayed there for three nights. I lost a considerable amount of weight as my mouth filled with ulcers, much like that of a cancer patient receiving chemo. I could not swallow properly let alone eat. I started to feel guilt if I even had the smallest thing.

Someone commented "you look like you've lost weight". It clicked, and not eating was the way forward. Why hadn't I just done that before? It was my key to achieving the body I knew I wanted, I dreamed of, I needed. My appetite left due to the fever, and I was vulnerable to the eating disorder I did not know I had. My diary entries read:

"I like being in hospital, people come to visit me"
"I'm starting to feel a bit thinner for first time ever!"

On discharge I was extremely tired and eating very little, maybe a yoghurt a day. I was still on Christmas holidays from university and arranged time off from my part time job. It's hard to recall what happened in the following weeks, except that my clothes became looser and people commented on my shrinking frame. I would go days without eating then despite my fear of food I'd gorge on sweets, chocolate and biscuits at night.

"I've eaten so much... lost weight but now I'll put it
all back on by eating crap...I'm so stupid, this is my
chance to be perfectly thin!"

It scared me but as long as I knew I was getting thinner, I felt okay. I judged my weight loss by tracing my fingers over my now delicate, now protruding, bones or I put on once neat fitting clothes and watched as they slipped from my tiny frame.

It was now February and this was one of the six months of the year I was allowed sweet food. I had a compulsive rule which meant that they were banned every second month. It had been a rule for as long as I could remember. As March, and the stricter dieting loomed, time to eat the foods that were probably keeping me alive was running out. Mum grew concerned though, as my appetite did not seem to be returning like the hospital had said it would, and I was fading before her very eyes.

"Mum says if I keep not eating I'll be anorexic, is that true?"
"Mum says my body is like an anorexic that doesn't eat food... even the stairs are hard to climb...but I'm still huge!"

Numerous visits to clearly blinded doctors left us with a cupboard of high calorie supplement drinks that would never go near my lips, I would put the straw in, place my lips on it and when a back was turned I would pour the contents down the sink.

"I just want be a size 6, then I'll stop losing weight"

I guess mum realised something was not quite right. It was Easter time and everyone in my family had bought me an Easter egg – I guess, in an attempt to encourage me to eat. Mum came into my room with a huge egg. My reaction was tears. I cried and told her I wished I could eat it but I just couldn't. At this point I felt some fear ... was I really the one in control?

The doctors simply said how it was a symptom of the glandular fever, but I knew something different was going on. I did not believe I could be anorexic as I thought that they NEVER ever ate – I was still having a tiny amount. I scoured the internet, finding information on all sorts of eating disorders, ticking the 'checklist' boxes, but then brushing off the 'diagnosis' just as quickly. I was surprised to read a diary entry from this time saying:

**"Think my life will just be a mess forever if I don't
become anorexic and then recover"**
**"Think this is the lowest I have ever felt...researched
anorexia, I tick so many boxes...I need to talk to
someone"**

I was just trying to get the body I wanted. I wanted the attention to continue. I still saw myself as too big. I thought if I could just get thinner I would feel lighter and have more energy. I did not think about the seriousness, or the affects of not eating. I felt fine, so why worry? But I wrote:

"Feel I'm so easily annoyed and feel really dizzy!"
"I can't think about anything but my body and food"

I was losing weight, going to the gym five times a week, but still eating the sweet stuff. It's strange I was scared of 'normal' foods like fruit and vegetables. It seems a bit backwards now. The opposite of how someone with an eating disorder would think, or how I would even think. I never ate during the day, only at night. I was too scared to start eating incase I couldn't stop. At least if I ate at night I knew it would have to stop. Bedtime would come.

Mum decided to take me on a much loved shopping trip to Glasgow. It started fine, but I refused to eat every meal. I happily ate a full pick 'n' mix at the cinema, and then even finished off mums when she was full. I really do not know why I could eat sugar and calorie ridden foods, but nothing that struck normality. As I tried on clothes, mum adamantly said that I would not be remaining at this small size. Why? In my head I had to get thinner. The worst part of the trip came the next morning. Mum wanted breakfast, so we went to a tea room. She had a lovely smelling plate of scrambled egg on toast. It was something I had never even tasted, but craved so much as I watched her put forkful after forkful into her deserving mouth. I sat with an unopened bottle of water. I must have screamed out 'anorexic' to onlookers. I could see the hurt in mum's face, but I was unable to put it right. I felt desperate, scared and confused. I felt powerless to what my mind was making me do, or not do. I could not stop thinking about food; it was my every waking thought.

Next, March arrived and the sweets and chocolate left. By this stage I was quite underweight, having lost about a stone and a half, and I had just started a university placement at a primary school.

Every day I was questioned by the other teachers about how frail I looked and why I never ate. I would watch them gorge in delight at home made goodies and sandwiches, as I sat shivering in the corner, wishing I could run and hide. The feeling of cold was like nothing I can describe; as though my bones were made of ice. I devised a plan whereby I filled a coffee carrier with diluting juice and told them it was full of a supplement drink from the doctor. 'To help me recover from the glandular fever'. They bought it, I think. Mum too believed my stories. The drinks never made it out the front door! Their thick contents would slide down the sink and their packaging, wrapped in tissue, would invade the bin.

I was down to drinking a single small low calorie yogurt drink each day, exercising and managing a class of 26 nine and ten year olds. I'm amazed at my own ability. I do not know where the strength came from but I coped, as anorexics seem to do. I coped too well, except for one day, when I broke down from feeling so physically ill. Words I did not want to say about the situation almost slipped from my lips, but I caught myself in time, and I lied. I said I thought I had a bug, but really I'd overloaded on laxatives the night before. My stomach was cramping, my body crying. Laxatives made me feel lighter. I abused them but paid the price in pain. Looking back I think it was more of a strain than I like to remember:

"If placement was not over in three days then I think I might die...god I'm a mess!"

I would manically crave food though. In my diary I would have endless lists of the foods my body was being deprived of, the foods that I knew I could not allow myself to eat. I wanted bread, nuts, crisps, coleslaw and sweets. I would have killed for these foods but would have died to be thinner. I even dreamt of food and would wake up panic stricken that I had maybe actually eaten them whilst sleeping.

My placement ended, and more time was freed up to exercise. I don't think I ever really though about what was happening or where I was heading. I got into a routine, I felt I had to follow. It was not to be broken. I had rules of times and amounts of everything from food to exercise. If I exercised for two hours at the gym I could sip at my yoghurt drink. I was so unhappy I cried constantly and had suicidal thoughts. The food deprivation locked me in an, unknown to me, depressive state.

I stopped seeing my friends as I had little spare energy, so spent most of my time with my mum, my sister Karen, and my niece Bethan, who was luckily young enough to be oblivious to my emaciated body and manic mind. My evening revolved around television. I would take sips of my tiny drink while a programme was on but was never allowed on an advert break. I didn't question my rules, I just obeyed. I was obsessive about the way things were done and all the numbers in my life had to be even, even down to the number of sips I took. To this day numbers still rule my life.

Mum was getting really vexed. She booked me an appointment with her doctor. Little did I know that she had already spoken to her and told her about my situation. I was extremely reluctant to go. What was I meant to say? What would she say if I told her the truth? Was anything really wrong?

On arrival she said: "So what seems to be the problem?". I broke down. "I just can't eat". I'd never felt truly upset or scared about my lack of food but she seemed to hit a nerve. She made it all so real. She weighed me. I hated that. I hated someone knowing my number. It was simply never low enough. She told me that I had to start eating, get a blood test, and come back the next week. She handed me a slip of paper to give to the nurse who would take my blood. Her writing was scrappy and I could not make out what the reason for the blood test was. I stared blankly at it, I thought it said "anorexia" but couldn't be sure. I wanted to ask the nurse but felt too embarrassed. I think I almost wanted the label so I could justify what was happening to me. A reason to the way my life was spiralling into some mad world. I bought more laxatives on the way home. She'd been no help!

I was to return the following Tuesday. On the Monday I'd eaten some unexpected cereal, I was petrified my weight would shoot up on her scales, so I convinced mum to change the appointment to the Thursday. I went, only thinking of the scales. I couldn't have cared less what she had to say. To my devastation my weight was similar to the week before. I wasn't obsessive about the specific numbers up until this point, but she made it such a focus. Such a focus, that from then on, my world revolved around the numbers on the scales. Her words I will never forget; "How can you not have lost weight if you are not eating?". I felt like such a failure. Like she had this expectation of me, like she'd labelled me and I wasn't living up to it. I felt like I was nothing now!

From that moment on my aim was to lose more weight than I thought possible. Unlike my future weight losses, I didn't set targets or have scales I obsessed over at home. I just constantly checked every inch of my body each day for bits that would soon be gone – bits invisible to everybody else. To others I was already a walking skeleton.

The doctor referred me to the outpatient eating disorder services. I did not return to see her. Mum was the one who kept contact with her. Mum was becoming more and more distressed. She clearly needed a professional to talk to. I recall, at this time, being at a friend's birthday party. I felt eyes upon me as they saw a shadow of my former self.

"At kirst's party everyone was saying how much weight I had lost and how down I seem?"

I had not discussed my eating or the doctor visits with any of my friends. I found it hard to focus on the night as they drank and laughed. I cried to Shanon in private and told her the doctor thought I had an eating disorder. It felt all so real when I said it out loud, and I was scared. She said that people were talking about what was going on: how my frail body emulated one of an anorexic, that I should start eating to get back to being the old me. I don't think she quite knew what to say. It was an illness we had all heard of, yet never encountered, or understood.

Weeks later I insisted on visiting a different doctor as I hadn't been to the toilet in months and the small amount I was eating weighed like a brick on my frail body. She looked at me with a presence of shock. She demanded that I be admitted to hospital. I was confused. I could not comprehend her concern. She said she could smell ketones on my breath. This is when your body starts to eat its own muscle. It should have scared me but I was more worried about the threat of hospital. She weighed me. I was a stone lighter. She made a call. I was terrified. Surely no one would stop me now? I had still so far to go. I wasn't ready to stop. I did not think I would ever stop, I still felt too big. Mum was called into the room. They both fretted, but I was allowed to leave: me relieved, mum devastated.

I genuinely believed I was well except from tiredness and constant coldness. However, I did experience severe back pain. I would double over constantly, even in public, to relieve my pain. It was my kidneys; they weren't coping with the lack of fluid. My mood and emotional state were taking a beating.

It s a diet gone wrong...
1 m not ill

In the weeks following I started seeing someone from the outpatient eating disorder team: a psychologist, but I was so consumed by anorexia that her help was hopeless. She kept asking me about my family, my childhood etc. Now I understand that she was searching for the cause of my problems, but at that stage I though it was all about me just wanting to get thinner and thinner. I thought I had only had anorexia for two months, it wasn't until after a lot of intensive therapy, that I realised how long I had been ill for.

I didn't mind going to the appointments, in fact we were a week early for my very first appointment. I cried and cried to mum. I felt that I was so in control that I was losing control. I just wanted to talk to someone. I refused to discuss anything with any of my family or friends, so the appointments were my only chance to offload to someone who wasn't emotionally attached. I went to the appointments, but I was still convinced I was not ill. Mum drove me to every one. She would drop me at the door, to preserve my energy for walking up the flight of stairs to where I met my therapist, she would sit patiently in the dull waiting room, and then take me back home, as I acted as though nothing was wrong.

Straight away my therapist banned me from the gym, but I could not stop going. I was petrified not to. I needed to exercise. My weight was falling and she was concerned. She asked me to record everything I ate and drank in the week in a 'food diary'. I would sometimes eat the night I saw her then start the diary the next day. I was too ashamed to write anything down so I would starve until I next saw her. It was tiny amounts I was eating but the paper looked as though it was designed to be blank. I was so messed up. I even wrote down if I ate a tiny sugar-free breath freshener.

I can't actually believe the gym did not stop me from attending. I wore a full tracksuit so I guess I hid it well. I was so cold that even after exercising I could not remove my jumper. As I walked to enter the pool three stone lighter all eyes were upon me. Still I could not understand what they were looking at. I guess it was a fragile topic for anyone to bring up. There was another lady who worked out there. She was clearly anorexic too. I wanted them to stop her because she looked so frail and in pain, but I saw nothing wrong with my own behaviour. My own appearance.

At this time too my sister gave birth to my second niece, Eva. I hoped that some of the worry about me would stop and that the focus would be on her. I remember holding her in my arms as they all ate dinner together. She was tiny, but heavy on my weakening body. I cried to her as I fed her the bottle and wished I could once again be so naive and innocent. We took her into the shops one day to see Shanon. Shanon looked quite shocked at the change in me in only a couple of weeks. Later she told me that her colleges had asked what was wrong with me, did I have cancer? But still I could not comprehend.

My sister suggested that I take a photo of my body to see what everyone else saw. I remember looking in the mirror that night and for the first time thinking that I looked like one of those starving people you see on the news from Africa. My bones protruded though my pale skin, my chest was now flat, and my legs were like a child's. But this was not enough to stop me. I brushed it off like everything else. I still had this desire, want and need to keep to my routine, to keep losing weight. Eventually the gym ban came. I was relieved. Walking up stairs had become enough to exhaust me.

The suggestion of a hospital admission was brought up at each therapy session, but there was no way I could agree. I wasn't ill. I was just on a strict diet. But with nothing improving she eventually demanded that I be admitted to the city hospital. I was petrified but my anorexia was no where near as powerful as it would show in later years, so there wasn't so much of a fight.

I spent two long weeks on bed rest on an inflatable mattress, to avoid pressure sores. I was in a ward full of elderly people. I'd shake my legs under the blanket in my protest to no exercise. I was though naive and did not know that some people fight back, I wish I had never discovered that people fight back. I drank the tiny sips of high calorie supplement that they gave me and accepted a drip in my arm. I cried a lot, that's all I really remember. I do also remember that so many people came to visit. The wall beside me was covered is messages and cards, and flowers overtook the table where food should have been. I felt liked, loved and cared for. I started to feel better and believed that I could go home and, once again be well.

Little did I know that my therapist had other plans. She visited one day with the information that I was being moved to a specialised eating disorder unit in Glasgow. I was only to destroy myself more for years to come.

I had visited the unit the previous month with my parents. Against my wishes. I did not speak for the entire three hour car journey (there or back), nor when the ward manager spoke to me so positively about the unit. I hung my head lower than ever. I did not look up to see the bedrooms or dining room. There was no way I was going to stay there.

Mum cried when we were there, I suppose because of the realisation of how serious things had gotten, but I showed no emotion throughout the whole experience. I felt numb. What illness? I believed it was Vicky controlling me. They told me people stayed about three to five months … no way!

I was devastated. But off to the unit I went. Taking painkillers on the journey as the bones in my bum were so sore from sitting on the seats in the car.

Home Sweet Home

So I arrived at the place that would teach me to become the "best anorexic", that would teach that me that I had to fight for the title, that, no longer let me stay the thinnest or most 'special'. Now there were 22 others following the same path as me.

I was escorted to a room. I pleaded with mum not to leave me. I promised her that if she took me home I would eat, that I'd do anything. I begged her not to leave me there, a million miles away from anyone who loved me. But they left. They did as they were told. A patient, later in my stay, described me as a rabbit caught in headlights at this point. A shaking, crying, misunderstood 'child'.

I arrived a scared, frail, naive little girl, with a label hung round my neck. I was unsure of what it meant, I just believed that it proved that I was thin. Suddenly I was surrounded by other girls who thought, acted and felt like I did. Some of these girls weren't naive like me... they were experts. Experts in the field of anorexia...their eyes were open, not held shut like my own. Each day they slowly began to prise open my eyes, unshielding me, and introduce me to their world...anorexia loved it. There was competition and I was willing to play...I believed that the title of best anorexic had to be mine.

As soon as my parents left, two of the patients entered. They were soon to be my friends. I described the first in my diary as a skeleton. I had never seen someone so emaciated, and I did not know it was possible. She made me feel huge. Anorexia was fuelled, and told me I was not ill. The other girl was like a ghost. So pale and hallow looking.

I felt so out of place. At home I had been thin, but here I felt enormous. There were bones sticking out of the girls in places I didn't know we had such bones. I just wanted to run and hide. I tried to convince my new psychiatrist that I was not like these girls. I was simply on a diet that had gone a bit wrong, and that if he just let me go home he would see that I would be fine. I could not comprehend that it was an illness controlling me. It just felt like my thoughts, what I had always believed – that losing weight was the path to happiness and contentment. The other girls all seemed to have had things happen in their lives to bring on their eating disorder, I had not. I felt like a fraud. He had heard the pleas I reeled off to him, all too often. I was there to stay.

The next person to enter the room was like the devil to me. Well, to anorexia. She was the dietician. She asked what food I liked to eat...none. She asked what I would like to eat for my evening meal...nothing! I cried to her, "but I just don't eat". The other girls had already warned me that food was not optional here. BUT I DON'T EAT!! The first night I was allowed to have my meal in my room, unsupervised. I picked at a couple of vegetables before pushing the plate away. This would be my one and only chance to refuse.

It felt like an outer body experience, like I was witnessing this hell, but surely not living it. I lay in my new bed that night and sobbed at the insanity. How had I gotten myself here, and how the hell was I going to get out of it?

The next day I experienced the dining room. It was shared with patients from the other units too. It felt like there were too many people. I could not possibly eat in front of them – it was too shameful. The experience was bizarre. I was expected to just eat. No excuses. No preferences or dislikes. I had to just eat. Initially you sat at a table with the other patients, also at the start of their treatment and with a couple of members of staff who were there too, to monitor what you were eating, to check you were scrapping every piece of food and sauce off your plate. They were very supportive, yet strict when they had to be. There was no getting away with anything. I often wandered how they now felt about food, when each day they would watch us all make such a big deal about eating the smallest thing. I was very focused on what they had, and would be angered if they opted for a salad whilst, at the same time, I was forced to eat a plate full of carbs.

The girls stared with complete fear at the food in front of them. Their eyes never left the plate. A couple of them would try to initiate chat but mostly there was silence. Their heads were bowed so low that there was only about an inch between them and the plate of hell. I followed suit. I had forgotten how to eat normally. I had not eaten real food in so long. Never in my life had I eaten the meals we were given. Salads were out and creamy pasta was their replacement. I had been a follower my whole life, why stop now?! I needed to fit in.

I refused, but also physically could not eat all my food on the first day. The smallest bite felt like a mountain. They 'let me off' with some things but on the second day I was no longer the new one. Another girl had been admitted too, and had taken a really bad turn. The patient, now one of my best friends, had suffered a cardiac arrest; yes, that's a heart attack!

She was sitting next to me. I can still visualise her body as it went straight and stiff as a board. Any colour she had, vanished. As we were all rushed out of the dining room, I became even more terrified by this place. Patients were overcome with sadness and worry. I cried, not quite believe what had happened. Another patient hugged me and said, "It's not always like this". Thank god, I thought because I could not cope. Luckily the girl was okay. But after that 'incident', the rules became stricter than ever. I sat for an hour and a half eating my sandwich the following lunchtime, breaking our half hour eating rule. I was not getting to leave that table until it was gone. It was horrific. I remember it like it was yesterday. I felt such shame and pain at eating something so 'normal'. I could not even think of the last time in my life I had eaten a sandwich – years and years had gone by. Simply taking bites like a normal person would, was too hard, was too strange. I ate the crusts first, squeezed out the filling, and then preceded to eating the bread. This was to be the beginning of a lifetime habit!

How the hell could I be expected to eat an evening meal too? What I was given in there was more than I had ever eaten before in my life. But when your weight did not increase the recommended amount each week, which was two to three pounds, more food was added!

We were weighed three times a week: Tuesday, Thursday and Saturday. The panic over what the scales would say was hell, from the night before. The scales were digital, and screamed the numbers in red to you. I despised the thought of gaining weight and when I saw the numbers creep up I felt like I was dying more inside. I would write in my diary that I could not possibly stay there as my weight was getting too high, yet to them it was still worryingly low. Numerous times I was asked to wear tighter belts as my bones upset both staff and patients; I was blind to their concern. We were not allowed to discuss our weights but my friends and I would say: "bad day" if our weight had gone up. No more needed said. Other girls would see it as an achievement if their weight rose – they were recovering. Any increase in my weight destroyed me. As your weight increased you were granted two daily, fifteen minute staff escorted walks. I lived for these short outings. Rain was my biggest enemy as often walks were cancelled.

After each meal we had an hour of supervision to stop us exercising or being sick. It was in a room with a television and magazines. I would vigorously write whilst sobbing at what I had just consumed. You saw the depths of some patients' illnesses, when they would try to exercise or put their fingers down their throats, not caring that the rest of us and members of staff were able to see.

Lesson time

My anorexia showed her true colours in years to follow, but this admission truly taught me what anorexia was, how to be the best at it, and clearly how you were meant to cling on to it. It channelled all my thoughts into an even more weight and body focused world. I had never met an anorexic before. Again, I just thought an anorexic was someone who did not eat and was really thin.... someone similar to all the models I idolised. But there was this horrible competitive side to the illness, and I was getting sucked in.

I watched the girls and heard their stories about what they had experienced, the reasons why they had their eating disorders, and why they wanted to get better, (or often, did not). I was vulnerable and felt alone, but by being part of this anorexic community I was accepted. I felt understood for the first time in my life. I wanted to be and stay part of their world. I felt in no way now like an outsider anymore, we had too much in common.

"This place is home now."

My bedroom wall was covered in cards and messages of hope from home. I felt like people cared and was petrified that if I gained weight and lost the illness, that I would once again fade into the background. Filled with insecurity, I worried that I would have nothing, be nothing.

"I just want to be anorexic"

The girls paced their floors to try and un-do the thousands of calories they were made to eat each day. Legs twitched and shook as we sat in group therapy, pouring our hearts out with secrets and stories that were never to leave the room.

I had experimented with making myself sick in the past. The first time I was twelve and on a girlie sleepover. We ate so much that I couldn't cope with the feelings. When I started restricting what I ate, I rarely needed to be sick.

But the girls in the hospital would throw up food they had eaten hours before!

We would cut and dissect our food into the smallest pieces and eat at snails pace. Dividing my food into 'safe' and 'scary', I always ate the safest first and left any fluids until the very end: I feared everything and contamination to me meant enjoyment or normality. I started to adopt all the methods they used. Instead of getting 'better' I was developing more as an anorexic. We would cut out pictures of the most skeletal celebrities and plaster our diaries with them. I wrote constantly. I could not mentally cope with everything that was happening so writing became my release.

Recovery described as watching a flower grow, or maybe re-feeding a dying one. It's such a slow process but said to give an amazing and worthwhile result. Like the flower I do not feel like I was given the choice. I wanted to wilt away for a while, have a break and not have to stand

strong, but they've fed and watered me. Made me grow.
This flower is now physically well but is still dying on the
inside. It wants to wither away again. Why do I want to
wither amongst a beautiful bed of roses?...because my
petals don't feel or look as good as the other's. They're not
special or worthwhile. But people won't let the withering
flower die, nor me.

I cried constantly each time we spoke in group therapy as I discovered more about how ingrained my eating disorder was and how unable I felt to let it go. It was me. I began to realise just how low my self-esteem and confidence was and that it had been this way for so long: that this was what had inevitably led me to anorexia: it was not simply a diet gone wrong.

I even started self-harming. Again it was copied behaviour, but it seemed to click that I should cut myself as punishment for gaining weight. It was a cry for help and unfortunately got me the help I wanted. I remember being fourteen and seeing a lady who self-harmed in a magazine, I was horrified that someone could do that to themselves, but here I was, now doing it to myself too.

I rested my arms on the white porcelain sink. Blood ran,
dripped, and splashed from my once child-like wrists.
No longer was the skin smooth and perfect, it was now a
canvas of my pain. I have to destroy this body I hate. I'm
unable to move my arms as I decorate the sink with red
swirls. The blood feels warm against my ice cold hands,
I feel no pain...not until later as I lay down to rest do I
have a tightness like elastic bands snapping around my
wounds. The now scarring skin catches on my bed sheets. I
cry into a sodden pillow and question if tomorrow will be
any different?

I became extremely close to the other girls; especially Seonaid and Holly. We talked about everything – from skinny people, to how long it had been since we had or had not been to the toilet, to what we wanted when we finally escaped this place. They became my family, and my real family and friends were pushed further away. I did not think they could understand what I was experiencing .... these girls could. I was losing my grip on reality and 'enjoying' the life of an ill person, who seemed to be at a school for eating disorders.

I cannot deny that I had fun today with the people I used to be so close to. But I could not help feeling that our separation has caused a distance, a lacking need to be constantly together. Quite happy to return to the place I now call home. I'm safe here, everyone understands me. I'd rather stay here than continue with life. I cannot face rejection or judgement. I just need to stay ill!

The staff too became a huge part of my existence. I became too attached to them; they were who I could spill all my thoughts and anxieties to. They understood and comforted me. They made me feel 'special'. I felt that without them I could not cope. I formed particular attachments to certain staff and clung to them, refusing to talk to others. I seemed to choose those I admired and who I would like to be more like; they became some sort of idols to me. Being ill and in hospital transformed me back into a childlike state. I was eighteen, but growing younger by the second. I craved the staff's affection; like a small child would their teachers. On the outside world my friends were maturing into adult life, while the patients and I slipped back younger than our years.

The worst days were when new patients arrived. It wreaked

havoc on my mind: how thin would they be? Would they refuse to eat? Would they demand staffs attention? Would they be a 'better' anorexic than me? It happened almost weekly, one patient out, another in. However it soon became apparent that having one admission to hospital did not always cure you. Patients who had been in numerous times before were returning back, more ill than ever. It was sometimes better if they had been in before. At least they knew the rules and how it all went, but it was so sad and any hope I had for the future lessened.

It was recognised that I was quite depressed, so I was put on anti-depressants. I hated the idea of being on something that would falsely change me; I wanted to be the one in control. I believed that with medication, how I felt wouldn't be my true feelings. Admittedly they did improve my mood; it did not change my mind set but it did make living easier.

My mum who had been my rock throughout, somehow became an enemy. She wanted me well. I was told to get better for her and I was angry. I did not feel ready or willing to change and it was like she stood in the way of anorexia. I did not want to hurt her anymore. She had expressed such distress at me being ill and I hated it, so I pushed her away. I An extreme of what would follow in years to come when I clung onto mum resembling an infant. Would sometimes leave four days before I would call her from Glasgow. And even then the conversations were strained as I refused to talk about my treatment with her. I was too ashamed that I was eating, gaining weight and miserable.

"All I do is cry, I want to call mum but just can't"

I was described as 'ambivalent' throughout my admission.

One day I would be focussed and determined to recover, seeing anorexia for what she truly was, and seeing what she had stolen from me, my life. I would be adamant I did not want to return to my old ways – I wished to live and move on. The next day however, I would refuse to move forward. I felt scared at what life had to offer; I simply hated being me and couldn't accept the weight gain.

'A day in the life of Anorexia'
"Get up, get up you lazy shit". My eyes won't open. Part of me wanders if I'm dead or alive, the other part does not care. As I peel my tired eyes open, my cold bony fingers begin to check my body – my jaw line, collar bones, rib cage, my pride (the hip bones that protrude through my skin more than any other part), my stomach. My stomach .... panic overwhelms me. It is not concave as usual. What have I done? What the hell has happened? My mind races. I remember back to the night before. I had allowed myself some cereal. I try to fight the voice, "It's the first thing in three weeks", but the voice is stronger and punishment is the only answer...I roll my emaciated body out of bed, something cracks – maybe a bone? Who cares? Gym clothes lay waiting on the floor. I remove the clothes that saved me from freezing through the night. Tears roll down my cheek at the thought of the workout I'm about to do. As I move, watchful eyes are upon me. I ignore them and relish in finishing: feeling dizzy and faint ...I feel repulsed by my size. I rest in the sauna but the wooden beams bruise me. I get home. Mum's still at work so I lay on the floor doing sit-ups until she returns. If I lose count I have to start from the beginning. I tell her I spent the morning watching TV. As the evening draws in I do watch TV, but whilst tensing my body constantly .... I just need to burn more calories. The countdown is on ....only eight hours till I'm back in the gym!

It was decided that I should go on 'time out' towards the end of my treatment. This was a week away from hospital, at home with no support! My self-harming was getting worse. This was seriously frowned upon. My attitude towards recovery was far from positive as I idealised my anorexic life style, but I was terrified to go home; it had been so many months. I cried the whole car journey. I wanted the safety of the unit. At home I found it near impossible to eat like I did in there. My sister Laura became my biggest support, and so she would continue to be for the years to come. She sat and rationalised my manic mind but the voice inside was still too strong. I experienced panic attacks and still had the familiar desire to lose weight. Being back home brought back all the bad feelings of anorexia: tiredness, constipation and obsessions with food. It opened my eyes to the negativity of the world I was contemplating subjecting myself to. I felt I maybe needed to change. I spent the week locked in my room; writing constantly about my mixed up feelings:

"I wish I was back at the unit. I hate home!"
"Hate to admit it but I need food, it gives me so much more energy"
"Don't go back to anorexia, deal with things and learn how to cope alone and accept."
"Mum made me have breakfast, only did it for her and because I'll have to do it when I'm back at the unit"
"went for a walk at the beach, such a contrast to the last time when I couldn't even walk because the wind was too strong for my weak body"
"thoughts of food are horrible, I hate having an eating disorder"

'Letter to my Eating Disorder'
What have you done to me? The list is endless. You've stolen away so much of my life, made me totally consumed by you, made me believe that you are the most important

and the only thing I should ever think about or focus on.
You convinced me that life would only be perfect with you
in it...but in your eyes there's no such thing as perfect. A
target weight once reached, only change. Keeping everyone
out, your power was fuelled...I was weak and unable to
fight you. You revealed bones you had wanted to show for
so long, and you put me on a treadmill to death. You were
so strong that I could only see and hear you, everyone else
vanished. I was famously fine...I was never ill enough...was
your intent to kill me? Was that how far you would go? You
pulled me so far from those who loved me...I hated you but
relied on you...I feel nothing without you yet you bring so
much pain...can't you just leave me alone? Are you me?
Are we one?

On return to the unit I had lost weight and really struggled to get back to eating. But I felt I was home. I was safe. Instantly I forgot about the rawness of anorexia. She convinced me she was my saviour, so I lied: I said I was focussed and determined to recover, simply so I could stay and avoid normal life.

"Everyone is so happy to have me back, I'm glad to be back at the unit, I'm so attached"

My admission lasted eight long months. But by the end I did not want to go home. I felt safe in hospital, had become used to it, and did not want to have to face the outside world in, what I saw as, a horrific, fat body, though now it was simply healthy.

"I cannot cope leaving the unit; I need the patients and staff. I want to tell dad to turn the car around and take me back there"

I developed in the unit, and made progress in some ways – mostly by gaining almost four stone, but my mind remained a mass of anorexic thoughts and both staff and my family were doubtful that this would be my one and only admission. I had already started losing weight on my weekend passes home through restricting my food and exercising. I stuck to the rules while I was at the hospital but had less control over my anorexic mind when I was at home. I was told to remember the bad parts of my illness, and to stop looking back on it through 'rose tinted glasses'. They had given me the tools to cope at home but I was unable to flick that switch in my mind.

Deja vu?

Each time I returned home after a long stay in hospital there was a slight buzz about being back. My friends saw only the healthy looking exterior and not the overpowering mind. I hated the body I had been left with. Emaciation expressed my distress at being me, this body did not!

"Think my friends think I'm better, I'm not, and I'm on a weight loss mission"

Anorexia I need you back! I miss you so much and I can't cope without you. I hear your distant yet familiar voice calling me everyday, and you seem like you're getting closer. I've stopped fighting you, I have realised that I'm not ready to let you go. I wish we could be together in secret. It's hard though, everyone is aware of our friendship and our actions spark danger in other's eyes. I feel lost without you – a nobody. You numbed the pain I feel. I preferred that. Given the chance I'd turn back time and not have ever met you. I would have just experienced freedom like others do, but you came into my life and taught me so much about myself. You've given me so much, but sometimes I wish you weren't there. I either have to fight you (anorexia) or long to have you back. Now I've got you I can't seem to get rid of you, I've forgotten what it feels like not to have you there. You feel safe and reliable, even though you're probably the most

dangerous friend: I know your power and what you are
capable of making me do.
I'm alone, caught between two worlds: one which consists
of you and me together and another, the real world. I hate
the real world; ours has so much more appeal. I'm locked
in depression. Maybe I was before but you numbed me
from it. I seriously cannot cope. I hate this life, but it's my
own self-hatred that is making everything so bad.

When I lost a certain amount of weight I allowed myself
out and about, but not a minute before.

"Laura.F's going shopping for black clothes for me; I
cannot wear any other colour and cannot be seen in
town"

Beyond belief I felt shame at my new form. I was heavier
than I had been my whole life. Even when the weight
began to fall I still could not face public places. Two of
my friends offered me to freely shop in their clothes store
after opening hours, but anorexia threw it back at them,
saying I was too fat. I could only wear dark clothing as
'she' told me I'd look slimmer.

One day mum took me for a walk to the bank; I made her
take the longest most detoured route in order to avoid
traffic or anyone who may know me. I was so ashamed
and disgusted by my body, I felt truly repulsed. I had never
felt thin, even when I was at my lowest weight, but this
was horrendous. I could not make sense of it – anorexia
was meant to get me the body I wanted, not the complete
opposite. I would cut things out of my menu plan each
day. I always said I would eat three meals a day, but I was
cutting so much out that my well intended promises did
not last. I was falling deep into anorexia's grasp.

**"I inhaled the smell of their lunch with jealousy as I
ate only an apple"**
**"Shanon said I looked thin again, I don't think so but
I'm so glad she said it"**

When I had lost weight I would hit the town and drink like a normal teenager, but little did everyone know that I would go home and slice at my arms with a razor to punish myself for the smallest thing that might have happened, or for simply being the weight I was. I was not a happy girl.

**"Considered jumping off a bridge tonight... Sliced my
arms with razor, my friends don't care about me"**

I was lost in my anorexic, depressed world again, very quickly. I felt alone. It was after my first admission that I met my therapist Emma. She was to have one of the biggest impacts anyone has ever had in my life. She had knowledge not only in eating disorders but very quickly of me. She burrowed deep and discovered the core of my illness. I insisted she weighed me weekly as I needed to know how to control my week's intake. I just wanted the numbers to fall. I wanted to undo what eight months in hospital had done. She soon cottoned on to my plan and refused. She felt was in my best interest but it only led to me buying my own digital scales which saw me weighing myself daily.

**"Tested out my new toy, the scales, I'm down four
BMI's since leaving hospital"**

Each day as I saw the numbers fall I got sucked more and more into my anorexic ways again. I would pace my bedroom floor religiously from morning to night, I would hide food, and I began to refuse to eat or drink in front of anyone so that only I knew what I was consuming. This led my family, and especially my mum, to yet again, watch me fade away.

"Home a month, eating in private, scared someone saw my lunch on the plate. Touched food as unpacked shopping. Mum praised me but I was just exercising"

I've been stolen away from her. Anorexia has captured me. I need to be told what's wrong with me and only anorexia tells the truth.
I can feel mum's hand reaching out to me. So often I feel as if I could grab hold of it and fix everything that I have messed up so badly, but her hand is met by a sharp pain. Anorexia uses me to fight her off. As I glare, ignore or close the door on her, anorexia nods her head in agreement, as I go to shout sorry; my lips are covered by the bony hand that guides me through my existence. I must not disobey. I am her follower. She wouldn't make me do wrong – she only cares about me.
Almost immediately I am whisked off into my anorexic world to further discuss and debate weight, food and exercise. I leave behind the person who wants me, as anorexia does. I'm out of mum's reach. Her fight is not as strong as anorexia's. Anorexia hits back ten times harder, building unbreakable barriers. Mum promises me love, while anorexia promises bones and hope. I wish mum could be with me, be happy for me ... but she just doesn't understand. Anorexia wants me all to herself. Mum angers anorexia. Mum wants me free of my closest friend, the one she describes as the devil. She pleads with me to let her in, and to give her, her little girl back, the little girl that was so often called her favourite. Silence is how I respond to her innocent plea.
I've ruined her life as anorexia tries to perfect my own.

I'm too big to be mum's child right now. Once I've shrunk down she'll see how happy I am and will be glad I never listened to her. Anorexia only wants to help me.
Mum wanders why my friends are allowed closer than she is... the truth is that I won't hurt them by being honest. They don't know anorexia's power, so we can laugh through the seriousness of the situation. Their constant focus and worry is not me.

Eight months of therapy had maybe saved my life, but it had also now made me live a much different one. One with such strict and harsh rules, new behaviours and new plans. If I missed out some calories one day, they were never to be added back in, if I paced for ten minutes extra at night I would have to add it in every night. It felt 'normal', but I was, at times, extremely distressed. My mood was slipping and the horrors anorexia brought filled my existence:

"Totally exhausted. Absolutely no energy. So, so cold. The slightest movements are the biggest effort. Feel low and very hopeless"
"Is it possible that my days are getting worse? This is no life. Maybe I need hospital but just can't do it"

I was freezing constantly. I literally had no warmth in my body. I wore layer upon layer of clothing but nothing could heat me through. I would slice my morning apple into a million pieces before heating it up in the microwave. I tried anything for warmth. I wanted the pain to stop.

This is my plea (anorexia) and I hope you are listening. Please will you promise me that you will stay? Please don't shrink my body down and just leave me feeling exhausted and low, irritable and isolated. I trust you and believe in you because you are always there, waiting to catch me, as I so often fall. But I do not think I could cope with the same misguidance as last time. We were left stranded, left for other people to pick up the pieces, to tear us apart. I was given the chance to leave you but you convinced me that you had changed your ways, that this time the plan was to be different. But already I feel tired and low. I want to push you away if this is my future, but my wishes are wasted: to kill you would be to kill me. My life revolves around you. I try to envision the future, but you keep the blindfold so tightly knit across my eyes. All I see is you. You paint vivid pictures in my mind: ones where I'm skeletal, dressed in clothes I can only dream about, surrounded by friends, feeling happy and carefree, cared for. I know this did not work last time, people refused to sit back and watch. Do you keep pushing me until I break or does the day come when you untie the blindfold, loosen your grasp, pat me on the back and say well done, can I achieve what you want?

I had so many rules and regimes, my life was totally engulfed.

There are rules you have to live by. Abiding by them is essential if we are to stay close and together, away from others who simply do not understand. You accuse me of changing the rules, but it's only to keep you on your toes. I only punish you if you are starting to slip. I only care about you.

Everyday you must sit not lie, stand not sit, walk not stand, run not walk. In other words never rest your body, keep moving constantly. Stay productive at all times, don't become fat and lazy. Your bedroom is where you should always be, door closed and isolated, until you have lost enough weight to be shown. Anything could happen if you dare leave. It's only time to rest when the hands on

*the clock tell you. As you pace the wooden floor ensure
your music plays to drown out your footsteps. The TV
must never be on, that's laziness. Both feet must step on
the rug: right then left. Your room should be immaculate;
this cannot be another area others can criticise. Don't
allow anyone in, they'll spoil it.*

*Keep checking your disgusting body...use eyes, hands
and mirrors. Dress only in dark clothing to hide it.
Wear nothing too fitted or in anyway revealing. If you
really have to leave the house wear "the jacket", it covers
everything. Cut off all clothing labels, until you have
reached the size of a child.*

*Do not let your family in. I know their strength, the bad
influence they have on you, the way they make you feel
about me. They want to steal you away and banish me.
Fade into the background with your friends, for you have
nothing to offer until the bones reappear. I'm all you have,
soon you can flaunt me. You can only see them on nights
out as this will give you an excuse to exercise by dancing
and miss meals the next day.*

*Where the most rules apply, where you get it wrong: food!
Each day we are aiming for less than the day before. I let
you eat, simply because we cannot be separated again,
we need to keep others off your back. Have nothing high-
calorie or in any way 'treat-like' as others will only think
you have lost control. When you eat it must be at home in
the privacy of your own room, no-one else must be aware
of this disgusting habit. Always concentrate solely on the
food – not on what is going on around you. Never sit-up
straight, look directly at the food, analyse it. Have nothing
touching on the plate. It has to be mechanical .... it's not
for enjoyment. Eat each 'section' separately, including
fluids. If to my dismay there is any part that you find
more bearable than others, definitely do not leave it
until last, we do not want the memories in your mind or*

your mouth. Eat slowly – slower than others would. Tiny
mouthfuls. Remember: eat less than everyone else.
Don't worry, take my hand and I will guide you, the rules
are just there to help! Love from anorexia.

Emma was extremely supportive, but sadly I was not interested in her enthusiasm to recover. All I cared about was losing more weight. I just wanted her to listen to the torture of my thoughts without standing in the way of me reaching my goal. But this was not what 'therapy' was about (so I was told, all too often), so she made the decision, a hard one I'm sure, to stop seeing me. It cut me and my family up. She was like our only lifeline and now she was gone.

I've lost the ability to smile or cry. My face is closed and
distant. I truly believe that I no longer want to live, but
I'm unsure of if I really want to die. I spend days wishing
I was dead, yet fearing dying. Please don't let go of me
Emma. You are what keeps me going, the only one who
understands, understands anorexia. Like anorexia, I feel
you will catch me if I fall. I don't know if I want caught
but I want you. I long for the next time I see you as I live
my life in such isolation. I need to discuss my world with
you, and for you to listen. But I can't give you all you
want from me. I understand your reasons for leaving, but
do you understand what you are doing to me? I'm scared
I'm destroying my mum's life, but without you I feel there
is no stopping anorexia. It seems like 'her' perfect excuse.
I think of where I have come from, to where I am going. I
shrunk the body, grew the body, I hate the body and still
I am left with me. Should I have lied the first time we
met in order to keep you close? Should I lie to you now?
Should I hand you everything that is me: anorexia? I
want you, but you will never have 100% me. I am owned

by anorexia. Like a child I want to cling on to you, but a child I am far from.

Consumed with anorexia I just accepted her leaving me and moved on. We all knew where I was heading; straight back to the place I had been nine months ago. I remember seeing Emma about a month later. She looked shocked and saddened at how ill I had become. Anorexia was now no longer bringing me joy and excitement. It was hell.

The threats of hospital started to return. My consultant said that if I did not change my ways or agree to go in then they would section me. This terrified me. It meant that all control would be taken away from me. I could not handle this threat so I agreed to go back to the unit, missing a second all girls holiday to Cyprus.

"I have agreed to go into hospital so I'm not eating until then"
"I'm no longer eating, I'm surviving on 2 calories of diet coke a day, it's the only solution"

It definitely took its toll on me:

"So tired, feel dead. Feel faint and ill."
"Scared I die"
"My breathing feels funny. Shanon took pictures of me in my bikini, she said it was too scary to even look at me. They did show a lot of bones, but I'm not thin"

But this admission did not last long. I did not want to be there and my actions and words made it very clear to both staff and patients.

"The staff asked if I wanted to get better... NO!"

I would cry constantly and exercise excessively in the privacy of my room.

"Called mum, I just want home. It's too hard here. I don't want to gain any weight"

I was oblivious to how sick my mind was. I could only think how ill the other girls looked. My ill mind was screaming to others:

"Elaine said out of all the anorexics she has worked with I am the illest, I feel a horrible feeling of pride"
"I don't want to die; I just want to lose more weight than ever"
"I want to kill the dietician for adding in a supplement drink"

Elaine was a leading eating disorder Occupational Therapist. She spoke words of truth, but I failed to register her concern. Anorexia saw it as a tick in the box. I lasted a mere two months before discharging myself against medical advice, to the shock, horror and fear of my mum. I was no longer naive. I was running the competition and wanted to win! Mum also discovered the true horrors of my self harm and I believe she crumbled even more.

So I left hospital with a low BMI, I was dangerous in others eyes, but too heavy in my own mind. I had a BMI I wanted to get to and no-one was going to stand in my way.

You're what ?

The next two and a half weeks were truly amazing. I am sure that is hard for anyone to hear but they were. I barely ate anything, drank very little, but I felt elated. I was losing weight faster than ever, was constantly active, and I was living. I was out with my friends all the time; shopping or partying. I was enthusiastic about life and mum would have described me as 'a pleasure to be around', not the depressed soulless girl she had become used to. I didn't think too far into the future, unlike everyone else. I just took each daily weight as it came. They probably feared I was going to drop down dead any minute, trying desperately to reach an unthinkable weight. As I said at the start; I felt invincible. I felt that anorexia and I were skipping hand in hand, and that my happiness would only grow, the more those numbers on the scales fell. Looking back at my diaries it was not all plain sailing:

"So cold it's unreal"
"Dreamt of food last night"
"Threw my sandwich outside to the birds and got caught, shit!"
"Body starting to look thinner"
"Went out clubbing, all I could think about was my body, and how tired and faint I felt"
"My legs are in agony from pacing constantly"

My consultant believed I was eating 500 calories a day. I felt so clever that I was only having 47. I guess anorexia was just kidding me. It was clear by my now tiny frame that I was not eating. My bloods showed a serious deterioration in my health; my body wasn't coping and was starting to give up on me.

The day I was sectioned came. One of the most horrifically memorable days of my life. The day that would lead me to being my illest. From the room with my consultant, I ran in fear, only to fall into the arms of two nurses who were 'luckily' coming to escort me to hospital. I was literally dragged across the car park to a locked psychiatric ward. One hell of a scary place.

I cried uncontrollably. I was meant to be having a friends birthday party the next day. How, I thought, could it have all gone so horribly wrong? I felt betrayed, punished by my consultant. At that point, as far as I was concerned, he had ruined my life. Now I see that he save it.

I was put on 24hr constant observations, which basically meant I obtained a second shadow - someone who never left my side and watched my every move.

I was so angry and scared of the section that I refused everything. I refused all food, and only took tiny sips of water. I did this only whilst hiding in the corner of my room so that no-one would see me except my shadow. I felt so ashamed of even drinking. I was desperately trying to be the one in control, I saw everyone as the enemy.

Whilst in the privacy of my bathroom I would photograph my naked body. I wanted proof that I was thin. I felt the bones, saw the bones, but I was convinced I was too big. I would do sit ups on the concrete floor, bruising my back; soon the door was to be left open. I would try to pace the floor at times but I was weaker than ever. It made me feel so lazy, but my body was fighting against anorexia.

"Feel so ill, my insides are in pain. I actually had to sit down, I just couldn't pace"
"Chest feels tight, I'm a bit worried"
"My weight is too high but I can feel all my bones. Back in pain, cold, exhausted and low. I was so much happier at home"

I stayed in the ward for a week like this before becoming so weak that I collapsed in my attempts to exercise. My body could not take any more. I was convinced I would have been fine if they had just left me alone. But now I know that I would have died.

I was moved from the ward to the city hospital with the inflatable mattress. One of my best friends visited straight away and was shocked at the fight I was putting up against the doctors. I just didn't want their drips and tubes. Her text later read "Do you want to die?". I felt guilty. I think she was just angry. She probably thought I was being crazy. I was so scared of anything entering my body though. I was terrified of gaining weight, so even the fluid drips horrified me. I was concerned that I had not seen what my weight was in a couple of days. I slipped into a serious depression. I saw anorexia as my lifeline, my reason to live. Without it I would be left an empty shell, what I did not realise was that she was killing me.

"In hospital with a feeding tube. Parents upset but I feel numb, angry, down, and so blank. I tried to pull the IV drip out. I hate this"
"They told me I'm in this bed because it's next to the cardiac arrest alarm, I don't understand, I'm fine!"

I had only ever seen one girl being tube fed before, and she had told me how horrific it was. It seemed like such an unpleasant experience but horribly I felt it made you look more like an anorexic. Clearly my emaciated body was not enough for anorexia. A tube was put in almost immediately and not long after I pulled it out. It was a long thin tube, inserted into my nose, down my throat and into my stomach. It hurt going down. They used KY jelly to help 'ease' it down, but I refused incase it had hidden calories. You were meant to drink water to help to help it slide down the throat: I again refused, meaning it had to be pushed through force. I could not stand the thought of being fed this high calorie poison, it was killing me.

We went through days of battling - the tube would be inserted by staff, only to be pulled back out again by me. It angered and frustrated the doctors and nurses. They did not understand anorexia and had little time or patience to deal with me. I was threatened: "if you pull this out one more time we will stitch a tube into your stomach". The thought appalled me. I felt like it was a kick in the face - what the hell was I meant to do now?

The feed ran 24hrs a day; I had no break from it. So I started tampering with it in a desperate attempt to limit the amount of calories entering my bloated body. I pierced it with earrings, and pins from my cards. I would make a small opening to let the feed run out, and onto my bed during the night. I still had my shadows from the psychiatric hospital, but any chance their back was turned I would switch off the machine. Usually they noticed straight away but I once got through a whole night before my 'achievement' was discovered. I felt like I was being clever, but I was still so miserable.

"I am writing to myself as no-one else understands.

The distress I feel is unspeakable and indescribable. I do not think I have ever felt so alone and distressed...I don't trust these ass holes...I'm so fat... the noise of the feeding machine is killing me...I want to cry but just can't"

I felt so fat and lazy just lying there. I would hang one leg out the bed and shake it uncontrollably in a last attempt to burn off some calories. I was desperate to leave this hospital. Though I knew I was not going home, the other hospital seemed more appealing. Here I felt hated and powerless. Three and a half weeks later I was allowed to leave.

"It's like prison - guards surround my bed, my life, my existence. I hate them all. If I died today it wouldn't matter and my life would have been shit"
"I cannot fight anorexia, so why are they trying to force me, stop wasting your time"
"Going back to psychiatric ward, three staff came and basically held me down so I didn't run away"

I dreamed it would be better but it was more hellish than ever. I had my own room but that didn't drown out others' screams. The ward was mixed with a large variety of mental health problems and so fights broke out daily. I had fights of my own. I began once again to pull out the tube in protest, any chance I got. It would take about five members of staff to restrain me to get it back down - a very unpleasant experience. I would smother my face in my pillow so they couldn't reach my nose and once I was turned over I would clamp my jaw, push my tongue back, in an attempt to 'close' my throat. My frail body was bruising from my struggles.

I had gained very little weight during my time there, much

to my surprise, maybe a kilogram or so, but it was agreed I could have set walks up and down the corridor. These were my saviour and probably the only thing that kept me from insanity. But like everything else I abused them. Sometimes my shadow would follow me, but sometimes they would just stand at the office door chatting. This being the case, I would turn my walk into a high powered run with jumps at the end. I must have looked crazy to onlookers, but I couldn't have cared less. A bony girl with a tube hanging from her nose doing some massive workout. Mum refused to visit or allow anyone else to, when I was walking. It looked too painful. My weight began to fall. From then on I had to WALK, wheeling the feeding machine along side me. I was distraught. Other patients would comment on how much 'better' I looked since coming in. As ever I took this to mean that I had gained a huge amount of weight. I would storm away crying. No reassurance from mum, that it was just the observation of a return of colour to my cheeks, undid their words.

"I'll die if one more person says my face looks healthier…I know I'm fat!"

I cried manically and was becoming more and more suicidal. I could not cope with the power the section had over me. Anorexia could not cope. I just wanted back to my anorexic ways.

"Feel like I'm failing anorexia, I'm so bad…I need to show them my real identity, I should fight more, but what if they take my walks away?"
"Don't forget, don't change, cling on, fulfil what you want, don't let those bastards win!"

I believed I was being punished in the most horrific way.

I had more anger inside than I thought was possible. I had never been an angry person, but my eating disorder brought out a rage in me I had never seen before.

Visitors outside my immediate family were banned, as staff said they would 'exhaust me'. This decision infuriates me to this day. I lost my friends when I probably needed their cheery faces more than ever. Without my friends, I slipped further into the arms of anorexia and depression. Being locked in that ward I lost all hope for life and sanity. All my lights were turned out.

My tampering with the tube, and not agreeing to 'plans' brought punishment. My possessions were taken away. First to go was my mobile phone, my only link to the outside world, to friends and support from the girls I had met in hospital. Seonaid and Holly had been through similar experiences and therefore worked hard at keeping me positive, even though they were both struggling themselves. I was losing all connection to the outside world. Festering in this ugly room, with its blank, dull walls and mould was enough to destroy anyone's optimism. Next to go was my MP3 player; used purely to drown out the sound of the feeding machine, staff and other patients. Eventually everything was returned to me as their game did not seem to have an impact. I was not going to go along with their rules and that was that.

I had one regular visitor, my assigned social worker, Susan. She was a blessing in disguise. I did not hold any anger towards her like I did to the other staff. She was genuinely so caring. She allowed me to offload my distress. I was a mess. No longer that well presented teenager I used to be. I was scruffy, pale and my skin with peeling through lack of nutrition. I feared her leaving. I felt safe when she was around. I wanted her to stay. I have little recollection of how our conversations went. It was probably me pouring out my mess of anorexia and depression. It was not until later years when I was managing a little better that she admitted to me that I was the most cognitively impaired person she had ever met. I was all eating disorder. There was no Vicky left. I was consumed to a degree I can't even write about. She said that her and her team doubted I would ever recover from such a state. I had no other thoughts, no space or time to think about anything else. This hospital had no stimulation for my manic mind and the staff were not trained as they had been in the specialised unit .... the specialised unit .... so it was there I was to return.

Me again but not Vicky

An ambulance was arranged for the long journey, and mum pack my bags, with little agreement or participation from myself. The night before I left I pulled out the tube in a frantic rage. It was re-inserted but much later when staff had eventually calmed me down. I slept very little that night; I was barely sleeping anyway as the constant feed kept my mind too alert.

A nurse I hated and a nursing assistant I loved accompanied me on the journey. She held my hand the whole way and wrapped me in blankets: Lynda was her name. Along with Meg, she was my rock in that horrible place. They spent countless hours with me. They couldn't break the mould anorexia had set, but they cared for me no end. I shook my legs and panicked about what lay ahead. I knew all too well the rules and regimes of the unit, and I was petrified. I felt I looked pregnant from the weight of the feed in my stomach and was scared at what staff and patients would think. I believed I was huge, yet my clothes were slipping off.

When we arrive, I tried to run away. My attempt failed and I was dragged up to the ward, to a room right at the nurse's station for all to see. It was called an observation room but we patients knew it as the goldfish bowls. Only the most ill were put in such invasive rooms.

I cowered in the corner of the small room as doctors and other staff came in and out. I was iller than they had ever seen me. The girl that joked and smiled through her pain no longer existed. This girl was hollow and suffering.

I believed this admission wouldn't be dissimilar to the ones of the past. How wrong was I? They knew how big a fight I had been putting up so decided to land me with another shadow. They had to be within arms reach of me at all times. Whilst some of the staff were courteous enough to stand just at the door when I used the toilet, others stood over me. Stage fright? I think so!

I had arrived in the afternoon, but before I knew it, it was dinner time. I had paced my floor the whole time. I felt they were unable to stop me here unlike in the other hospital, it was an exhausting but necessary process. The meal came and went – untouched, I even refused to eat the calcium tablet they prescribed, convinced that it would make my weight rocket for the scales the next day. It had been a while since I was weighed and I feared the worst, as always. With a fight, water was put down my tube and once I had paced for another four hours I was instructed to get into bed, I was relieved that someone had stopped me, my body was weak, but my mind was still so strong.

"My mental state is all over the place, all I can think about is anorexia…my head is in turmoil and I need out"
"Marissa said she has never seen me so ill, that I make no sense…I'm exhausted by my thoughts"

They came with a bag of feeding supplement to put through my tube over-night. 'No way' I thought. I had seen the other girls. They were tiny – feed them, not me! I was so pleased, however, to see Holly's face. It reassured and comforted me that there was someone I knew, and someone who knew me. She seemed to be doing so well. She was one of the illest people I had ever met; if she could break free then there was hope. I got away with taking my feed on the first night. After the trauma of the day, I guess they feared for my heart. I got away with it that night, but those to follow were not so pleasant or peaceful. Each night I would pull out the tube, have to be restrained to get it put in back in, and then have my arms held down so I could not keep up my side of the fight. More than once I was given an injection in the bum to sedate me. It was so scary. I would go from a frantic beast to a sleeping zombie.

I refused every single piece of food or fluid they put in front of me. It had been months since anything had passed my lips. I actually did not have the ability to do it anymore. It was an alien concept. The longer I went without, the scarier the prospect of eating or drinking became. The sight, smell or touch of food made me feel sick. I no longer dreamed about it, I was only disgusted by it. Anorexia saw food as failure and I feared disobeying her.

I became an enemy to a lot of the girls in the unit. They saw platefuls of untouched food leave my room, identical to those that they were forced to struggle to eat. I felt guilty for my behaviour and its impact on the others around me, but the guilt was not enough to make me change what I was doing. When it came down to it, I wasn't there to make friends.

"The girls all hate me, I'm so alone"

I had little time for friendships. I had to pace constantly, which also angered the patients. Pacing was seriously frowned upon, but I wasn't there through choice, the section had put me there, so I wasn't going to stop. I was never allowed out of my room. I existed within the same four walls, with my shadow. I was so angry at everyone and everything. I hated the fact that I had to be there and had absolutely no control over anything. I hated the dieticians for always increasing the calories in the feed and for trying to force me to eat. To my disgrace I even became quite violent. I kicked a table over on her and on another occasion bit a nurse who was trying to stop me from pulling out the tube. It was clear that there was a line in their tolerance ... and that I was crossing it. I just seemed to lose all of Vicky and became this anorexic monster. I no longer cared about anything. I could feel the guilt deep down but anorexia was so strong that I would have done anything just to cling onto her.

"Please don't take away my low weight, it's all I have"

I was still vigorously writing my diary and stories of my pain; I also made a scrapbook generated around the section and the hell I felt that it was bringing me. I look at it now and see how negative it was, at how it was all me against those trying to help. I felt I was being punished for my 'choice' of a way of life. I was so lonely. I just wanted someone to collude with me, to reinforce that anorexia was the way forward; this obviously was never going to happen.

"I'm just a section to all of you"
"I need anorexia, not them!"
"Miss mum too much"

I loved my therapist, Lee. I became, as always, too attached to her. I hated when she left at night and loved the fact she came in early every morning. Each weigh day, three times a week, I would catch her on the way into the office and cry uncontrollably. Telling her how horrific it all was and long for her to help, to put a stop to this nightmare. I was not improving cognitively, but her reassurance and support was invaluable. For a long time my weight did not rise, it even slipped as I paced so much. I was accused of vomiting... "how?" I would scream, you watch my every move. My room was searched a lot.

My weight did start to increase. through a process of five members of staff holding me down four or five times a day; reinserting a tube and quickly pumping high calorie feed into me. It was a worst experience than ever before. I could not stand the thought of weight on my body.

It's so unfamiliar yet now so consuming. The emotion has wrapped itself around me. It peaks as my bare feet anxiously step on the all too familiar scales. The numbers flicker as usual before resting at a point where I think my legs are no longer going to be able to hold me up. I grab the handle of the door; someone asks if I'm okay. Are they for real? Did they not see what I saw? The anger erupts inside. The breaking down in tears comes later – for now frustration rules. I scream, pace the floor, punch the wall .... I'm like a caged animal. I don't know what else to do. The feelings are so strong, so intense. Destruction is all I can think.

Each day the same angry feelings follow me like a dark cloud waiting to explode when need be. I'm angry at the staff. What the f*ck are they doing to me? Life saving measures that are making me want to die! Each day they pull anorexia more and more away from me. I'm angry, so angry at what they are doing to my body, my pride, now my enemy. I have nothing. I am now nothing. Their army is stronger than mine. They have broken me. I am angry that I cannot stamp my feet and get my own

*way. I'm exhausted with anger. I want them all to piss off,
to take an interest in someone else's life, not mine.
I feel no anger towards anorexia, just to them. Why have
they put me here? What are they trying to achieve? Do
they want me to kill myself because surely this is what it
feels like to be dying!*

I was exhausted and emotionally drained after each feeding
episode. I would scream, kick and then sob hysterically
once it was over. Almost always, I would call my mum.
I was calling her about eight times a day. No longer was
I pushing her away, I wanted and needed her as close as
possible. I wanted her to save me from this madness. I
longed for her visit each Sunday. I wanted only her. I was
like a baby needing comforting. I suppose this was better
than rejecting her but she soon expressed to staff what
an emotional strain it was. They became strict towards
me calling her so often, or at times of such distress. I felt
a love for her like never before. I wanted her near and
panicked at the thought of her ever leaving me. This was
a reoccurring phobia I had about anyone who was really
close to me. I feared them dying, but yet I made them
watch me slowly kill myself.

Gaining weight was horrendous. I would have rather died
than gained weight.

*I want to disown you, I hate you. As I lay powerless in bed
in the early hours of the morning, a nurse held down my
arms and legs as I pleaded for them to stop feeding me. I
glanced then stared beneath the covers as I saw the once
concave stomach rounded as though I was pregnant. As
she held my arms, I feared that she felt the fat that had
replaced the bone that had been so prominent before. Later
I stand in front of what will make or break my day: two*

*tiny steps and a flash, the numbers appear and instantly
I crumble my head near explodes, I cry. Anger is what I
feel. I cover my body whilst pinching it, running my fingers
along that bones that I feel are disappearing. As I leave I
walk past a gaunt faced shadow, barely covered up, I see
what I wish was my reflection. I shudder at the thought of
my own body. I struggle to shower and dress; each area is
bigger than it was the day before. I tell myself that I cannot
feed this body again today. But as the day progresses my
body grows by the second. As it grows my connection to
anything and everyone fades, I can no longer face what I
am becoming.*

So I found any means possible to express this. I started
self-harming again, by getting my hands on anything sharp
whilst my shadows back was turned. It always happened on
a weigh day. It happened like clockwork. I would turn my
back in the shower for two minutes, slice at my arms, and
on cue for them telling me to turn round, I revealed the
massacre. They were generally superficial wounds, unlike
the ones in the years to follow, but never the less, my arms
were a mess with scars. As blood flowed from my wrists I
would apologise for my actions, but justify them with my
words of distress. No-one could understand how I kept
managing to do what I was doing, whilst under such close
observation. A second shadow was added. My room was
constantly searched. I was suicidal and everyone knew it. I
expressed to my shadow and therapist how I wanted to die.
My anorexia had become me and without it I did not want
to go on. In one of the room searches they found twenty
tablets that I had been spitting out each night. I hadn't taken
them as I knew they were designed to 'slow me down': both
in my mind and my pacing. I was unhappy yet terrified of
changing. My eating disorder was telling me to follow it,
while others were just trying to help me. I was throwing

everything back in their faces. Medication was thereafter put down the feeding tube: with a great fight.

"I'm like a zombie on these new tablets, it's horrific"
"They are not letting me feel anything, just drugging me up and making me fat"

I know now that the medication was essential if I was to be helped, but it infuriated me back then. It made me sleep constantly. I could barely move and at times could not even hold myself up. I felt as though they couldn't cope with my erratic behaviour so just fobbed me off with a lethal cocktail of drugs to get themselves an easier life. The situation was serious, and they threatened to send me to another hospital, with a room that would basically be just a padded cell. They needed to keep me safe, but I did not care. All my possessions were taken away from me. Anything that they thought could be a danger was taken: my straighteners, jewellery, belts and craft work. To this point I was still presenting myself reasonably well. I had my own style and decorated myself with accessories and was forever doing my hair. But they striped me bare. This punishment, alongside the weight gain and self harm left me distressed in baggy jeans and a hoodie, wearing no make-up, and left with messy hair. I was unrecognisable to my former self. I was a depressed hollow girl and every inch of me showed it. This truly distressed my family too. It was as though I was slipping further out of their reach, out from normality.

I've hit such a low. I feel as though my heart and sole have been ripped out, leaving me with a shell to exist in, and to hate. I've had enough of this so called life. It's only an existence. What the fuck is the point to it? Each day I wake to the same reflection, and the same horrific

situation. What the hell is the point? Why don't I just stop
it now? Surely I have the power to do that? Others control
every other part of my being, but life or death is surely
my choice? I hate that it has come to this. I hate that this
is the path I have been led to, the situation I have been
manipulated into. There's no pleasure or joy, just torment
and pain. I want to hurt me; punish myself for what's
happening. I blame them - they put me here. I did not want
to die before; I do now. I have lost all connection to life.
I'm not the girl that cared, that lived; I'm a shadow of my
former self. I hate all the fuckers who are killing me. It's a
slow and painful death. Set me free: I know you are scared
that anorexia will kill me but look what you are doing to
me, locking me in the deepest depression. Just leave me
alone before I do something we will all live to regret.

I slowly began eating as I wanted the tube feeding to stop.
It was making my weight go up faster than ever. They only
agreed to stop the tubing if I could prove that I could eat
everything on my meal plan. PROBLEM - there was going
to have to be a cross over period where I was doing both.
It was a double battle. One of the hardest things of my life.
I wanted the control back but it seemed like such a high
price to pay. The calories in the feed alone were in the
thousands, so eating too, would mean disaster.

"My head is totally fucked; feed and tube is too hard, I will fight back"

It started off small, with a quarter piece of toast at breakfast,
or some salad at other meal times. It was torture but with
encouragement and through sheer determination I began
to manage. Anorexia's words were fiercer than ever. One
of my main supports through everything was Linda. She
became my adopted mum. She was a nursing assistant and

did not have a background in eating disorders. But she cared about me so much, so her presence was enough to calm me during some of my worst times. She'd encourage me. She ignored anorexia and searched for Vicky. She was my shadow as often as she could be. Once, she worked thirteen twelve hour shifts in a row, just so she could be with me. She was so important to me, and entertained me with stories from her own hectic life. Me and mum both trusted and respected her. She was a rock to both of us. I think mum always felt more assured when she was on, unlike when agency staff were with me. Nurses that had never met an anorexic before were sent in to 'help'. They commented on how big my meals were, and told me how they ate nothing but salad ... helpful? I think not! I hated them. It was torturous enough to eat, but with a complete stranger who cared little about you, it was hell.

I remained on constant observations for months. Stuck in that same room, gaining weight, and making no cognitive progress. I spent Christmas in that room. Mum and dad stayed over at the nearby hotel, and tried to make it special, but because they left to spend the rest of the day with my family back home, I felt more alone than ever. I just wanted to be back with them all. I was more tortured then than when I arrived. Now a healthy body but a very sick mind. I guess I hadn't reached the point where I though: "Anorexia is serving me no purpose". I believed in her and believed that being thin was the only trait I could ever be recognised for. The tube remained in without feeds for a while. Until they were positive I would not refuse to eat. I don't really remember how I managed to start eating. I think I just realised I would never leave if I didn't.

"I want to die. I hate you all. I need anorexia back. I need free of this place. I need home. I need death. My weight's so high!"

Even when the tube and my shadow were removed, I was still in a place of hell and everyone knew it. I was granted weekends home, but I had to be collected and returned by my parents. It was an exhausting and very trying time for everyone. I, along with everyone else, had little hope for what lay ahead.

"A weight can depict your mood so much when you rely on it to hold your worth"

After seven months I was discharged. I had reached my target weight and had a plateau in my thinking, which was similar to when I arrived. I said that I would never be back forced back to the unit. I made it my promise, whilst knowing that my main aim of going home was to lose all the weight AGAIN. I wanted to lose more than ever. I was so trapped in my thinking. Being sectioned had forced me into an improved body, but mentally I was in no place to recover.

"My head is screaming at me, I am screaming at me, anorexia is screaming at me. I cannot break free; I'm suffocating in my own soul"

Mum says they did it to save my life. This I can see, but how dangerous it is to feed someone to a weight they can't or wont maintain. I felt more determined to, yet again, punish my body through starvation. I had a hope that I could finally find the happiness and the contentment I longed for.

My smile is broken, tears frozen, my eyes droop and my heart sunk. My once bright face has turned to a glare. A dazed blank expression of hopelessness and depression. I'm lost in a world I am struggling to see my part in. I

*continue to exist, not live. This seems my fate; my choice.
I stay in my box, wired barriers protecting me from
everyone and everything. I see no reason to laugh, but
every reason to cry. My thoughts race and my lips are
sealed. I've lost all connection I had with people. There's
a blank canvass, but there's no interest. My body screams
to show my identity but is masked by others attempts to
set me free. Wounded skin depicts the distress of having
to be me. The light at the end of the tunnel is darker than
ever. I'd run if I could, but I'm trapped. I'm stuck with
me wherever I go. I go to move but I am paralysed at
having to be me. No time to relax or stop, yet nothing to
do. As others move forward I step back. I shield myself
from the life passing me by. When I rest my head at night,
please don't make me have to wake. I scream in silence,
my mouth is too tired to open and a sound is to difficult
to make. I tear pages from a book as though chapters of
my life. I'm lost. I live away from reality, yet so far from
fantasy. I feel I am just waiting to die.*

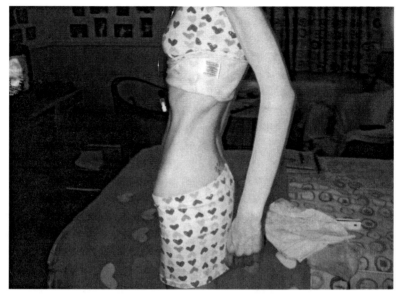

admitted to hospital after a week in the general ward

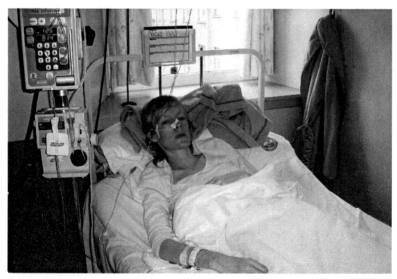

the day i collapsed and was admitted to medical ward

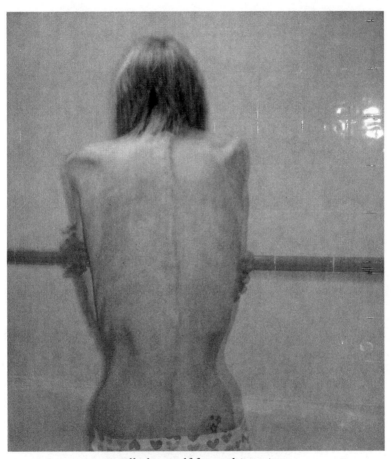

i called myself fat at this point

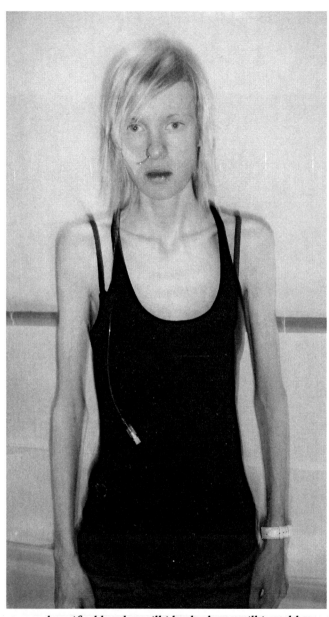

mum was horrified but how ill i looked, yet still i couldnt see it

A collage of my illness and feelings

Here we go again

The next few months were basically history repeating itself. My families' worst fears were coming true once again. I was back to cutting out parts of my menu plan and losing the weight I felt forced to put on. Everyone's best efforts hadn't been enough to quieten the controlling anorexic voice in my head. I paced more, and drank and ate less. The same targets were once again in my head and I was once again determined to achieve them.

I thankfully started seeing Emma again. The one person who completely understood my eating disorder. While she was recovery focused I was back on a path of self-destruction. I spent hours alone in my room, pacing and writing. I had so much going on inside my head, but Emma was the only person I would speak to about it, so I wrote constantly. I would panic if I wasn't always busy. My head deemed me lazy if I slacked in any way. I was existing. Far from living. It was exhausting, but the willpower and strength anorexia brought me kept me fighting. My behaviours were obsessive like never before. I had set times to eat and drink, they had to be stuck to. I feared if I ever broke my rules that my weight would rocket. It does not make sense. I did not make sense. But anorexia is not logical.

Things continued on this way until one morning I got up. Mum had gone to work. I was home alone as I was every morning. Mornings were my chance to exercise freely. I would go walking for hours on the old railway line where I was out of sight of anyone, and if it rained I would run manically around and around the house. That morning, I poured out my tiny amount of cereal and milk, then felt the room spin. Taking a tiny spoonful, I felt faint. I called my sister in a panic. I thought I was dying. I threw up in the bowl and collapsed onto the table. Mum sped home, and later told me she expected to find me dead. Luckily she was wrong. I moved onto the sofa and mum watched in fear as I slept. When I woke I felt fine, and was adamant that I needed to go on my morning walk. It was part of my routine, and I was petrified to break it, no matter what. Mum pleaded with me not to go. It was torturous seeing her so distressed, but I had to do it. She accompanied me and to my anger as she did not allow me to walk the whole route. I was devastated. I doubt my body could have carried me.

Mum called Emma and my consultant. I was to meet with them in the afternoon. I now couldn't see what the fuss was about. I felt okay. At the meeting everyone was very straight faced - clearly concerned. The words I dreaded hearing, came. I had only left the place three months ago and now they wanted me back there. Noooooooooo!

Without any agreement from me, it was arranged that I would return on the Monday to the unit. I was still sectioned so had no choice in the matter. It was Friday. I was determined not to go. Determined that they would have to drag me kicking and screaming...

"Suicidal thoughts so strong, think I may take an over-dose, I think it would be a cry for help, to say I can't go on"

73

Me and mum's silence in the car journey home spoke volumes. We were both devastated but for different reasons.

I remember planning ways of getting out of going. I even called the unit to say I wound not be coming. This had no impact. I had friends who were current patients there, and they told me horror stories of how competition was rife in the unit and how bitchy the place had become. I couldn't do another admission like the last time again. I needed out. I was learning a painful lesson - that people were simply not going to sit back and watch me fade away. My body too was suffering. I wasn't at my lowest weight but my body was deteriorating more than ever.

"I'm so exhausted...anorexia is crippling me to the point of total desperation"

So I planned an overdose. I wanted to die. The thought of being back in that environment and gaining weight was too much for me. I recall visiting my nieces and holding them extra tight as I said goodbye. I believed it would be my final one to them. I had never taken an overdose before so had no clue how many pills was 'enough'. I took all my anti-depressants, but carefully thought to leave out my anti-psychotic medication in case I didn't die. This being the case, they would make me too sleepy to pace. My thoughts were more irrational than ever, but I never told anyone of my plans. Maybe they could have helped if I had? I simply was petrified.

Mum found me still conscious, with the empty packets around me. It was the first time in my life I had ever seen my dad cry. Mum was surprisingly composed, but was sure to crumble later. She must have wanted to be strong. They rushed me to A and E and I soon lost consciousness.

I woke the next day, feeling very little in the way of side effects. I cannot remember how I felt waking up. Relieved I guess? This was a cry for help more than anything: my protest to going into hospital.

I was moved back to the psychiatric hospital. I thought, 'Yes! At least it's not the strict unit.' My consultant agreed that there was a lot going on down there and that I was best to wait a while before going back. It had to calm down before I was moved. My only thought was that this was extra time to lose more weight ... I took my chance.

I was made to take a tiny medicine cup of water every hour. I felt embarrassed if I had visitors as no-one ever saw me eat or drink. I barely spoke to the staff, though they did try to understand. There was another anorexic girl on the ward. Her tiny frame brought me such anguish about my own body. I felt spaced out most of the time, and exhausted. I could not pace. Walking to my bathroom was a big enough effort. I was wheeled anywhere I needed to go, which was generally no-where. As I lay on my bed I could feel only bones, but with no scales or mirrors anorexia led me to continue believing that I was fat.

I stayed there for a week, getting both mentally and physically more ill. I did not think it was possible for my mind to become more insane, controlling and demanding, but sadly it was. Mum once again packed up my things and an ambulance drove me to the place I seemed to be spending more time in, than home.

Take four

I was exhausted. I had eaten nothing in over a week, and had had very little fluid. I was dying. I was in severe emotional and physical pain. I had no energy to think, yet all anorexia made me do was think about her.

The walk from the ambulance to the front door (about five feet), was draining. I almost wished they had put me in a wheelchair. I was too tired. A familiar nursing assistant took me to my room. I broke down in a frenzy of tears. I could not do this again! I had no energy to cope with the mental strain it put upon me. I just wanted to sleep. A patient from my previous admission later said she had been too shocked by my deterioration to talk to me initially. She was angered no-one had rescued me, but how I had become was not from their lack of trying. I was not fully aware of how ill I had become, but I knew the anorexic drive was in full power.

The next thing I knew the duty doctor came in with a feeding tube. I couldn't believe it. I had not expected this. I was getting no time to settle in. They said that my lack of fluid was so dangerous that they would have to put water down the tube. They knew I would not drink. I felt powerless and soul destroyed. I could only think about being weighed the next day. I wanted it to be as low as possible and feared the fluid would stay in my body and increase the number. It was only water for god's sake, but I was distraught. My mind was a mess. Anything was too much. I wanted more than anything for the lights to turn on and to awaken from what was seeming like a horrific nightmare.

"Remember this hell. Never end up back here in this situation again. Kill yourself properly if you must!"

I fought and battled not to get the tube in, but I was weak. They restrained me every hour and pumped water into my skeletal body. I began to feel larger than ever. I cried hysterically down the phone to mum, after each ordeal. It was hell for her too, as I pleaded not to have this calorie free poison in my body. I was losing my mind. I wanted to die rather than to feel this extreme torment. It was like nothing you can imagine. I tried to pace but my tired body was struggling.

I asked the nursing assistant to take photos of me all evening. I wanted to see how I looked. And I wanted the memories, I would later use these pictures to beat myself up for gaining weight. The pictures she took shock me today. I see how frail I was. At desperate times I idolised the images. Those I have shown them too commented on the emaciation, but more so on the lack of sole in my hollow face. I look miserable.

That night they came with a bag of 'feed'. My distressed, however, out powered them. I pulled out the tube and was left the whole weekend having no nutrition apart from water. I was too weak to even lift my hairdryer and felt so faint every time I stood up. In the shower the room would spin and I would feel myself falling into the arms of my shadow. I believe I was dying, but still did not want or see the need to change.

Mum visited on the Sunday and was distraught to find out I had not been fed. She thought that that was guarantied here. I hated to see the sadness in her face, but I was too engrossed in anorexia to change.

The other patients did not really come in to visit me. They told me later that they were scared. Those who knew me couldn't believe how ill I had got, and the others only heard my screams, saw groups of staff coming in the restrain me, and saw full plates of food leaving my room. I was the patient that I dreaded in my first admission. The one who had totally lost the person they once were.

Starting on the Monday they once again fed me 'the quick way'. Like they had done the last time - holding me down and quickly pumping the high calorie feed into me. I was once again on constant observations and was not allowed out of my room. My shadow was back. Expected to eat along with the feed, I cried hysterically to mum, staff and to the patients who knew me. I would watch patients walk past my door and sadly started to use them as my 'thinspiration'. I believe I was enormous compared to them. I hate that this was the way my mind was working. These girls were in as much pain as I was, yet I was idolising them and jealous. I had become more ill in their attempts to make me 'better'. My image of my body was so distorted that I could only visualise myself as fat, no matter how low my weight was.

Weeks passed and I was fighting staff harder than ever. I just did not feel ready or willing to change. My mind was locked in with anorexia and depression. I truly felt I could not go without 'her', yet believed she would be the death of me: either through suicide or self starvation.

I had a new dietician this time. She was extremely strict and refused to listen to any of my eating disorder. I hated her for it. I would shout and scream, throwing my toys out my anorexic pram. But she started to make sense. She dug deep, hit the core, and rebuilt my torturous relationship with food. It wasn't food that was evil, it was 'her'. Anorexia. My dietician saw ME, and not the anorexia, and eventually I started to eat.

I started attending group therapy sessions and going to the dining room. They thought the pressure from the other patients might encourage me to eat more. It was a slow process but it worked. They were right. I felt extreme guilt watching the other girls eating whilst I point blank refused, so I just had to start.

I used every outing from my room to try and escape. I think it was my protest, yet it never worked. Someone was always there. One time, my shadow fell asleep so I crawled under her legs and made a break for the front door. I did not make it very far, but I chanced my luck, that was for sure. If I did break free I have no idea where I was heading. I wanted away from everyone and everything. My diary entries expressed nothing but anxiety, weight, and the need to keep on pacing and exercising for the months to follow. I can only imagine how infuriating this must have been for everyone. I was eating but anorexia refused to loosen her grip.

My shadow remained with me. I would spend my day texting another patient who was both on observations and the tube. We would be truly unhelpful and negative to each other; moaning about the feeds and weight gain. Our minds were as harsh as each others. Our illnesses seemed to bounce off one another.

I don t want her

The more chance I got to mix with the other girls, the more I saw how horrific my situation was. They had come in choosing to get better. They were the brave ones. I could see how hard it was for them and their determination shone through. I saw that the energy I was putting into fighting against recovery they were using to fight for it.

Eventually I started to make progress! Real progress! I stopped what I now saw as pointless fighting. No-one would let me live my life with anorexia. 'She' was only trying to kill me. The tube was soon removed as I was eating well, and my shadow faded away. It felt strange not having someone there all the time, but I embraced the freedom with a new kind of high. I saw that I had needed that person there to keep me safe and I needed support to win this battle. I started to feel like a different girl. I became close to the other girls. They became vital in my recovery. I even started to enjoy food and my thoughts were no longer consumed by it and weight.

"Had such an amazing day, feel so positive...I want a life"
"Friends are so happy to hear me so happy"
"Don't ever want to end up back here"
"Mood really good but body image is bad"

I'm not saying everything was perfect, but it was definitely an improvement from the years of hell. One day stands out especially in my mind. The ward was getting redecorated so the unit was taken out on a bowling trip. It was followed with the challenge of a two course meal at an American diner. I sat with my new friends. Their support was invaluable and we praised each other at the progress we were making. I was tired of putting up a fight all the time and getting no-where except from back in hospital. We would share our anxieties and our new hopes and dreams of better and healthier futures.

If we had laptops the hospital allowed us to use the internet. I joined the social network sight that all my friends belonged to and mended some slightly broken friendships. I would spend hours looking at my friends' photo's of holidays and nights out. Opportunities that I had missed out on. I came to realise that I didn't want to miss out on anything else. I now wanted more than anorexia; I wanted to be part of my friends. I needed a twenty year olds life; I did not want to be stuck in hospital anymore.

I lived for my weekend passes home. I vividly recall my first one. I surprised my friend Shanon with my return. We had dinner together, watched a DVD and even had sweets. Her sheer delight spurred me on in my healing. I would shop during the week with fellow patients, for an outfit for my Saturday night at home which saw me able to party hard with my best friends. They all seemed to be delighted I was eventually doing so well. They thankfully welcomed me back with open arms. I suppose the biggest progress was eating out with them, drinking alcohol, and not being consumed with the need to exercise, starve or self-harm. I was one of them!

My family too, especially my mum, for the first time in years felt there was some sort of light at the end of what had been a very long and dark tunnel. There was less need to walk on eggshells around me. There was no eating secretly or pacing the floor. They had Vicky back: new and, I guess, improved. Karen and Laura had their sister back and my nieces, their auntie.

The staff too expressed such delight in what was a transformation from the girl that had arrived. My therapist, consultant and dietician all played a huge part in helping me develop into this better person. They dug deep to the core of my problems but without my own motivation I wouldn't have got anywhere. I was angered at anorexia for taking so much of my life away. I was infuriated that I had not fought back sooner; but this was my time.

I was still not comfortable with my body now at a healthy weight, but for the first time ever I did not class myself as fat. I knew if I was serious about this recovery then it was something I was going to have to come to terms with. In group therapy we discussed 'body image' and talked about how to cope with everything our new lives would entail. It appeared that all the other patients had a positive attitude and it was seriously rubbing off on me.

I was desperate to get home for good and start living my life. My wish was granted pretty quickly. In the October, just in time for the Halloween celebrations, I left the hospital. I felt truly happy. I was bright, confident, and loving my new found freedom. Reflecting back, I would think: "Is it possible to remain this happy?". My recovery seemed almost perfect and I wanted, as always, for it continue this way. I was enjoying it and so were other people so why question it?

My 21st birthday was next. Shannon and mum arranged

the venue when I was in hospital. It was amazing. I loved feeling so loved. My friends made it so special. I loved my dress, and was amazed at how good I felt in it. I felt like I could put anorexia in my past and move on to live in reality. To live a life like my friends.

Time passed and I continued to stay well. Emma could not believe the new me, and for the first time, we worked together in my recovery. I started part time work, and my circle of friends expanded. Fashion was my biggest passion, and so working in the clothes shop with my new close friends was amazing. Things seemed almost perfect. My confidence and self esteem bloomed. In the background, however, things were not quite so rosy. I found at times I was eating when I had not planned to and it felt a little uncontrollable.

It was only ever 'small things' I added in, and I thought, 'that's what my friends would do'. It did not affect my weight so I ignored it, though there was something bigger looming...

My self-esteem seemed bruised as I felt something missing. I felt that if I had a boyfriend I would feel more loveable, so each night out became a search for Mr Perfect. This led to situations I would rather not discuss.

Around this time I started to doubt my sexuality. I was devastated, thinking that everyone would reject me. Thinking, 'Why me?'. As if I didn't have enough to deal with. Things were difficult so I made the conscious decision to return back to my anorexic ways. I see this as ridiculous now, but it was the coping mechanism I was so used to. This would be my escape. When you're weak and fighting to live you don't have to think about relationships. It was the security and comfort I needed.

Mum was all too aware of this dip in what had been such a pleasant mood. But I told no-one of my hidden feelings. She was desperate to re-capture the girl she'd had home for the last three months, so she offered me a holiday. A holiday to anywhere I wanted to go ... Anywhere!

I chose New York. I knew the trip was a bribe to stay well, and guess what, it worked. I pushed the sexuality thoughts to the furthest corner of my mind and looked forward to what was a trip of a lifetime, to a place that holds so many dreams. It was remarkable. Mum and I rekindled the relationship that we once had; we were like friends instead of carer and sick child.

But there too I felt I was eating too much. I was craving food. Walking a great deal, and being caught up in the excitement of shopping allowed me to brush aside my anxieties. I remember being in the car on our journey home from the airport and secretly eating a small bar of chocolate. It scared me like nothing on earth but I felt compelled to do it. The shame it brought crushed me. I had not planned to eat this but felt I had no control over my body's actions. This 'secret eating' was laying a path for the years to follow.

Summer sun

Back to reality, I'm not exactly sure what started to happen. I started self-harming again. Mostly after nights out, when I would come home drunk, single, and was worrying about my sexuality. But I still let no-one know. Emma, my sisters, and some of my friends knew about the self-harm, but not my reasons why.

Food started to take over. I found myself eating with little control and not really being able to stop. It wasn't so much binges like I would encounter in the future, but I knew it was more than I needed. It only happened about once a week, but it was bad enough for me to cut my arms. These were not the superficial cuts like in hospital, these meant having to go to A and E to be stitched up. They left scars that will loom forever, fade but never leave.

Summer arrived and I had two holidays booked. I had missed out on four all girls holidays, so this year Shanon was going to show me what I had wished for. I was excited but soon to be devastated. I had a miserable time.

On the way, Shanon told me that she did not eat a lot on holiday due to the heat. I hoped that I would be the same, so to look my best in my bikini. But no. My appetite seemed to be spurred on, and because we were drinking each night I felt increasingly hungry. Because she was not eating much I felt embarrassed and ashamed by my need to. I would buy food in secret and eat, hiding in shame. Food became the forefront of my thoughts so I had little room for enjoyment. I didn't feel like partying or socialising. I just wanted home. I knew I was gaining weight, so for the last couple of days of the holiday I refused to remove the clothes on top of my bikini. I was sick with worry and knew I was ruining both our times.

Shanon bonded with our neighbours but their presence only reminded of the horrors of secondary school. The guys were cool and confident, and I felt like a 'nobody'. Shannon's beauty had guys falling over themselves each day and night, I felt so rejected. I felt like the ugly tag-along that no one cared about. I felt I had nothing to contribute to any conversation or interaction. I was too caught up in my inability to control my food intake, my low mood, and my ever increasing horrific body image. I had a boyfriend at the time, but a compliment would not have gone a miss.

Once thankfully home I told my dietician about these eating episodes. She did not seem too concerned and as my weight had not changed drastically - there was no need to worry. But I knew deep down that it did not feel right. I just wish I had dealt with it them then, and then maybe the horrors of the future would not have occurred.

I dreaded our next trip which was for a whole month to Thailand. I could not cope with her not eating whilst I over-ate, or the thought of Shanon being the centre of attention whilst I was left on the sidelines. I couldn't cope with my self-esteem or confidence taking another bashing. Luckily my worst fears did not come true. We had the time of our lives. To this day we laugh hysterically at some of the things we did and saw. Thanks Shanon.

My eating was much more controlled there. There was no bingeing as we were constantly busy, I was confident and reassured that we were eating the same things, and I felt relaxed and comfortable in that amazing country. It's the last time I remember feeling content for a prolonged period of time.

Too much

On arrival home I had three weeks before starting my new university course as a student nurse. I had a dream to help children in the way I had been helped by so many, but I also had a desire to lose some weight. I wanted to start uni looking slim, feeling comfortable, and feeling happy. But the willpower I once prided myself on seemed to have vanished. I felt I was back to the way I was at school: having 'good' and 'bad' eating days. I felt angry at my lack of control, and expressed these worries to my dietician. I told Emma over email as I could not face telling her in person. I was so ashamed that I was struggling to do the one thing I had been best at: restricting. They were both extremely supportive and I felt confident, when in their presence, that I could control the situation. But as soon as I was alone I experienced disaster. On these so called 'bad' days I would generally be eating bowl after bowl of cereal; dry or with milk. It seemed the easiest, most accessible food in the house. It was so easy to just eat without realising actually how much I was consuming. Too easy in fact.

At the same time my boyfriend of five months ended our relationship, right on cue for me starting uni. I was devastated, and not eating was my reaction. It was not intentional, I just couldn't eat. I was too sad. I was once again in a situation feeling rejected and unlovable. Anorexia was there to catch me as I fell into a depression of self hatred. I blamed myself for the break up, thinking that I was unacceptable, and that I was doomed to be alone forever. I hated him for ending it but hated myself more for being me. I wanted my life to be perfect in every way .... an unachievable goal. I was scared if I did not have a boyfriend, others would discover the secrets I held about my sexuality; something I was willing to go to any extreme to avoid.

About a week later I received some horrific news: Holly, one of my best from the unit had died. I could not believe it. I slept very little, cried constantly, and suffered horrific grief. I had known she was unhappy and struggling, but never knew it was this bad. It showed me the power of this horrifying illness. I felt extreme guilt that I had not been there for her, or done anything to have prevented this happening. I almost felt I didn't deserve the right to be as devastated as I was, as I had not shown her the love I felt for her. But we lived in different cities, I had been having such an awful time myself, I had been too wrapped up in my struggles, that to support another was not as possible as I would have liked. Nothing prepared me for her death. I was angered, however, that people suddenly expected that I would stop eating because of it. How dare they put this added pressure on me at such a time? I took comfort from the other girls who had known Holly, and together we consoled each other. Starvation was not on the agenda for me. I was back to eating again, and no matter how hard I tried to fight the urges, I knew I was bingeing.

The funeral was so emotional. She was only twenty-two and did not deserve to die. I wanted it all to be a horrible nightmare, as I'm sure everyone else did. I saw girls from my past: some well, some horrifically ill. It was a tough day. We all had eating disorders and all knew what a battle it was. We had to find a way to move on. I will never forget Holly. She had such an impact on my life. She was the very first person to ever speak to me in hospital, and was there for me no-matter how much shit was going on for her. I know how loved she was ... and still is.

University had to become, and remain, the focus of my attention. I had made friends and was quite enjoying this new focus in my life. But my eating was still causing me distress, and my mood took an almighty dip. I felt the high of being out of hospital had longed since dwindled away. I was back to being me - the person anorexia had let me escape from.

I started my first placement, but I was distant and could not focus properly. I was cutting my arms and Emma was becoming increasingly concerned as I spoke of thoughts of suicide and my inability to lead a 'normal' life.

A week into my placement Emma decided it would be a good idea, a safer idea, if I spent some time in the psychiatric ward. I agreed. I was so tired of this battle and was desperate for some sort of break.

I was admitted that day. I slept and cried. I once again felt lost and hopeless about life. I looked completely different from my last admission, but the sadness was back in my eyes. I began totally restricting my food intake. I believed it would make me feel better, happier. I would feel the same high as I had done in the past. I began to lose weight but my mood was unbearable. Friends and family visited. I could smile and break free from things while they were there, but I was tortured in my own company. About three weeks into my stay I was no further forward. I was lighter but my mood was heavier. I was using the staff more; talking, opening up, but again, I felt desperate. To this day

I am not actually sure what led to my next action. I think it was distress at my lack of improvement. I felt wretched and simply wanted to die. I had a vase of flowers by my bed; I stood on it to see the glass shatter. I picked up a piece and started hacking at my wrist. I kept repeating the line: "I just want to die". I had never seen so much blood escape from my body before that point.

I was found about half an hour later. Crying, weak, and covered, like the floor around me, in thick blood. I think we were all shocked. What the hell had I done? I was taken in an ambulance to A and E. Alone. No-one came with me and they did not bother calling my mum. I was petrified and felt totally abandoned.

My wrist and arm were examined. Just before the stitches were put in, they told me that I had actually snapped a tendon in my wrist, and would require surgery. I was shocked and petrified. A kind nurse came in and comforted me. She called mum. I was put back to the psychiatric ward to wait for surgery the next day. My wrist is still weak, two years on. The scars remain, and the cold brings tightness as if I tore at it only yesterday.

The staff were clearly disappointed in me and some were angry. I believe it was my cry for help, for more support, but this was the opposite of what was to happen. It was decided that I should be discharged. In everyone's eyes this admission was clearly not working. The thought of being this low and coping at home was unbearable for me and my family. I wasn't completely alone however. Angie came into my life. My support worker. She wasn't trained in eating disorders specifically but was armed with amazing compassion. We met twice a week out with the hospital: me with a diet coke in hand. She would listen to my stories of heartache, desperation, and my lack of

91

control over me. Along with Emma and Susan, she was a miracle. But due to unforeseen circumstances Angie had to leave her position: another lifeline I waved away. I was distraught.

I left the ward with weight loss as my main aim. I believed if I was once again skeletal people would have to look after and protect me, and I would have the one thing back in my life that made me so proud. I rejected thoughts about the past, of how horrific things had been, I just wanted to return to what I remembered as 'safe'. I forgot this so called safety had nearly brought me my death and ripped my family apart.

I continued losing weight on the run up to Christmas and was starting to look frail to others. The bingeing continued, not too regularly, but enough to stop my weight slipping as low as the past.

At the same time I sought comfort in a friend who I knew I could always count on, Craig. We had been in the same class from first to sixth year at school, and had always been somewhat close, yet we never mixed with the same groups of friends. We were both part of the school drama group and we were house captains together. We'd had less contact since leaving school but knew we were always there for each other. Craig started to visit regularly and our past friendship and closeness was re-kindled. My family found Craig a godsend, as did I. He had the ability to free up some of my head space and I even managed to smile through the pain when he was around. I was losing touch with my best friends so Craig's support was therefore invaluable.

Happy New Year   not

The New Year came and I was unprepared for what lay ahead. 2009 was not to be a good year. I was still not eating my meals, but at night I couldn't control this new hunger I experienced. I binged wildly. My body was no longer accepting my self-starvation. It was screaming at me to be fed. I felt lost without my anorexic power. I wanted to keep losing weight. I knew the only way for this was to restrict my intake, but this was not happening. My pride had always been in my willpower, but it seemed to have vanished. This was the start of inevitable weight gain. When my weight was falling Emma would speak about the slippery path I was taking myself down. Now I felt I was heading in the other direction. I was so ashamed. I felt a complete lack of self control.

Craig and I planned a trip to Edinburgh. I was getting a new car, we both wanted to do some shopping, and I needed a break from the craziness at home. Me and mum both worried about how my eating would be. My head was all over the place, I was self-harming and I did not know what I really wanted anymore.

I'm suffocating; there is no room for me to breath. I feel I'm slowly dying the most painful death. I cannot see a way out. I want to go back (to anorexia). Maybe then I'll

see a way forward. But I can't even do that. I'm tortured
and tormented by this screaming punitive voice in my
head, telling me how shit I am at the one thing I used to be
best at. Throughout the day I feel empowered and strong
that I can refuse food and get a buzz from following what
'she' wants, but then the evening looms over me. I'm soul
destroyed. Hunger invades and she's ready to pounce if I
dare slip. I want her so much, but she's such hard work.
She offers safety, guards me from what real life has to offer,
as she turns me back into to a child. But her protection
and existence comes at a cost; it's not simple or straight
forward. There are so many rules and routines. She's strict
and allows no room for slacking. I have to remember that
she can take over, she's all powering. Do I want to lose
friendships and relationships? But think of the body I
achieve; I love it! A skeletal, childlike image. No curves, just
bones. Then others will see the pain I feel inside. You will
see my weak body and know that I'm not ok.
But is it only me that thinks that I look good? But with
thinness won't my confidence grow? So here's my plan for
a double life: I don't need her to kill me anymore because
with starvation I crave life. To me it makes sense. So why
wouldn't I chose this life. I keep being told to find a middle
ground between starvation and bingeing, but I cannot. I
cannot trust myself. I desperately need to be thin, but how
thin, I do not know. It's all a guessing game. I tell people
I'm trying; yeah I'm trying – trying to be anorexic AND
have a life, university, relationships, perfection. I'm not
anorexic; I'm fat. I'm a fraud. I'm a disgrace. I wish I was
locked in a prison cell, no food, just emptiness. Just make
me ill again. Let my mind go out of control. I can't cope
with this hell: shit kill me now!

Mum was delighted to receive a text saying we were in a
pizza place having lunch. I do not know what made me

feel able to eat 'normal' food for the first time in months. It scared the hell out of me, but I was happy in Craig's company and wanted to act as normal as possible. But you know what? That meal was a huge regret. Yes, it started me eating my three meals a day again, but it did not stop the bingeing on junk food in between. So now I had even more calories being flung into my mouth. I sneakily bought sweets when his back was turned and cried in disbelief.

Our trip away turned our friendship into a relationship and we were both pleased. But inside I was experiencing a nightmare. Food became the focus of my attention. I was consumed by it. I was bingeing, and my weight was increasing daily. My binges had changed drastically from the small amounts of the previous year. I could not believe how much I could eat before I became full or worst still become full, but have the inability to stop. I felt constantly bloated and uncomfortable. I stopped weighing myself daily as I was so scared of the rocketing numbers. I ate in secret, sneaking to the shops to buy chocolate, cereal, sweets, and biscuits - things that I had once feared even touching. I bought enough to feed a family for a week and consumed it in one sitting. Mum knew about the bingeing so stopped storing these types of food at home. But that didn't stop me. I could think of little else. Bingeing felt like an outer body experience. It was like something possessed my mind and made me eat whilst in a kind of trance. It was automatic. Before I knew it I would be guzzling down thousands of calories in one go. Suddenly I would then snap back to being me, realise what I had just done, and crumble into such distress. I would often make myself sick. Sometimes I was too exhausted from the binges to even move. I was actually in pain from the amount I was consuming. I was extremely reluctant to tell anyone about these episodes but I now know that my situation was more common than not. Girls I had been in hospital with were too, experiencing the same nightmare. In all my time in hospital I was never warned or prepared for the possibility of such a turn in events. Binge eating was talked about, but I believed it to only apply to those individuals with that label on them. It never crossed my mind that one day it might be me. Staff never explained that such a high percentage of anorexics became bulimic if they did not fully recover.

With the increased bingeing came the increased self harm. I felt I needed to punish myself for committing what I saw as the biggest crime, I did not see it then as another form of my eating disorder. I just saw it as greed. My arms soon became a portrait of the pain I was feeling.

Uh oh a binge is on the go,
Get the blades ready it might be full flow,
It starts off with a thought, the one I should have fought,
Telling me to eat,
Now I sit and greet,
Why the fuck is my life so shit,
Would you blame me if I wanted to quit,
People laugh and people cry,
I just have to ask the question why,
Why do I smile when all I feel is pain?
I'm literally going insane,
Thought I was safe, I was ok,
But now all I need to say,
I hate this grotesque body so much,
It's too big for anyone to touch,
Sick to my stomach I now feel,
the skin on my arms I will peel,
I cut them with a harsh blade,
I barely feel the pain I've made,
So cut my skin in a straight line,

Then in my mind I'll be fine,
Hospital and stitched like doll,
Cause I've taken another fall,
Anorexia is what we have written here,
They look at me; I'm no where near,
They look confused, I feel ashamed,
On my mind everything gets blamed,
For eating is the biggest sin,
I just wish I'd put the bag of food in the bin.

Not only this but in January 2009 I took one of many overdoses: tablets filled my mouth and buried their way to my stomach. I lost consciousness almost immediately. I was out cold for days and terrified my family.

"Bingeing is out of control...I'm so embarrassed, ashamed and disgusted...just want to be thin again"

I was desperate. I could not cope with this drastic transformation from the girl that used to never eat. I cannot remember if I wanted to die, but I knew I just wanted to break the cycle; to stop eating so much. If I was dead or even unconscious, no food could pass my lips. But my plan clearly did not work. Within a couple of days I was sent home, after briefly talking to someone, and then hell was straight back on track. On days I had the strength to refrain from bingeing I survived basically on pepsi max and caffeine pills; emotionally, I only coped by abusing food.

At the same time I started my second university placement, but again my mind was not in it. I was drowsy all the time and spent most of my free time bingeing on biscuits from the kitchen. I would devour packets at a time. Bingeing made me so sleepy that I could never really focus on the job at hand. Also, being in a hospital setting was just a reminder of where I had spent so long. I did not feel comfortable. I was gaining weight so fast that hardly any of my clothes fitted me. I started detesting going to placement.

"I'm obsessed with food to the point of desperation... complete and utter hell, unbearable...this horrible beast rides up from within...thoughts are 100% food...I hate f*cking placement"

We spent a lot of the time in a small office and I constantly thought about food. I wanted to sleep through the mental exhaustion. I could not wait for each day at placement to be over. I felt everyone could see my ever expanding body and the scars beneath my jumpers. I took another overdose at this time. My mentor knew there were troubles in my life., but I received good grades so that helped me to hide how I was really feeling. I returned to university: I was bigger, but half the person that they knew. I slept through lectures and missed tutorials. I handed in my final essay of the year on the point of breakdown: I had to leave the course.

Goodbye forever

Emma was, as always, an amazing support. I lived for my Tuesday appointments at 10am. She understood my eating disorder so well. She had an answer and opinion to everything. What she said always seemed to click with me, even if it did not resolve the problem. In March she announced that she was leaving her position. I was devastated. I felt she was the only person in the world who truly helped me. Who gave me hope for the future. I tried to persuade her to stay, or at least to just keep me as her patient, but my pleas were wasted. Unfortunately for me, her decision was final.

"Thinking about Emma leaving is killing me...I refuse to let go...why am I always punished?"

I was lost now that she was gone. I felt I had no-one. I formed an immediate negative relationship with my new therapist and very soon after stopped seeing her. I longed to speak to Emma. I still do. I longed for her to help me out of the mess that was my life. My social worker, Susan, was the best replacement for Emma; she too understood me and my illness so well, so I sought comfort in her. I guess when I form a relationship that I truly respect and believe in, I feel safe. This is how I felt with Emma and Susan. My consultant was great but he had a more senior role; dealing with medication and such like. It was harder to talk to him about the finer details. I felt angry at her for leaving, and for abandoning me.

Usually my pen flows with ease. Little thought, purely emotion. No-one else is involved. It's a relationship with myself, but this is different. This is a different kind of pain. I often worry my mum will die, that I won't be able to go on; it's like this. You are a main character in this awful sketch that is my existence. You are who I think of at times of need. You are who others ask: "Well what would Emma say?" You are what stands between me and pure insanity. Without you I feel I will lose my mind. I can't stamp my feet, swear, act like a child to get my own way. Unlike my mum, you wont give in to me. This is out with my control and I cannot stand it. I'm angry and frustrated. I want to say: "How dare you leave me?", but I know you are not mine, that ours is not the only relationship you have. But do you know what you mean to me? Do you know how much I cry as I write this? I have always been hopeless at ending any kind of relationship. I want to cling on to you for dear life. I NEED you! I have had nine different hospital admissions and no-one really got me, no-one knew anorexia and me so well that they could dig deep to places that I couldn't even think existed. But you can, so why are you pulling the rug from beneath my feet? Why do you have to stop the one thing in my life I trust, that matters so much, that I would sacrifice anything for? I am not blaming you. I cannot imagine what this kind of job does to you. But I am so scared. I feel like part of my hope is dying. When you stopped seeing me before, I didn't care as I knew the pattern: I'd lose weight and be back in hospital, but this time I feel my life is literally in my hands. Each day seems different. The hell of eating ,the joy of other things. But who do I tell? Who helps? I don't want someone new, I want you Emma!

I was once again desperate, and destined to deteriorate. I was relieved my placement was over, but was lost and alone. It was then I pleaded with my consultant to admit me to the psychiatric ward. A strange request to hear from me, I'm sure, but I could not cope any longer. The ward was mixed and I knew how chaotic it may be. I thought if I spent a week there it might stop the bingeing and allow me to start moving on with my life. I felt I needed the support and safety of the staff. I even considered taking illegal drugs as I believed this would stave off' my appetite.

"So low and suicidal. I see no way out of this dreary existence...I'd rather die than continue this misery. What is wrong with me. Am I doomed to a life of depression and probably obesity!"

He was reluctant until I uncovered my mass of wounds, I was cutting almost daily.

I want; no I need your help. I need you to take all of this away. I need you to rid my mind of the demon within. I'm literally, it's literally eating me alive. I don't have a life. For so long it's just been an existence and I've had enough. I have no strength. I am so weak. Increasingly I spend my waking hours huddled under my covers drowning in my tears. Being awake has become too much and I feel if things do not change I'll search again for a permanent way to sleep. As I write I pace, much like I used to, but back then I was a shrinking skeleton, now I'm a disgrace. I don't even want to write the 'B' word (binge). You all know what I'm talking about. I am ashamed to sit here in front of you, wearing the same clothes I have done for days. I have to wear them - they are all I can think to hide this repulsive body. I shower and dress in darkness, and in bed I lie with my arms wide apart from my body, scared to feel the flesh. Mum is no longer allowed to hug this fat body. My arms are covered in scars. The old ones show the hell of the past and for each day I overeat, a new one appears. It has become my horrific routine. I eat until I feel too upset and ill, then I scar my body as punishment, tape up the wound and here we go again. Why can no-one take this away from me? Why do I have to live with all this shit in my head? I feel so abused. I need someone with me all the time, to keep me on my guard, to stop me from slipping, to stop this hell.

He agreed that I was to go in for a week before considering going back at university. I was scared but knew I needed help before I did any more damage to myself. I was apprehensive, again, as to what the staff would think of me, I was double the weight I had been in my first admission.

The week went well. Not perfect but okay. I managed to get my eating under some sort of control. Well, anorexic control, I was barely eating. My weight was coming down and I was using the support of the staff as much as they could give me. I had a couple of nurses I always liked to talk to and to who I became quite attached. They were not trained in eating disorders but they were incredible listeners and offered valid opinions from an outsiders point of view. It was only later I realised how dependant a person I was, and I had always been. I feared people leaving me as I felt abandoned.

"If I'm alone I cannot cope. If I don't talk to staff all the time I'll lose my mind...I feel hunger and this brings fear...I'm huge and insane - What is happening to me?"

I was diagnosed with Borderline Personality Disorder

(BPD). For me, this means I have severe attachment issues, and the constant dread that people are going to abandon me. This new and additional label scared me, but it made a lot of sense. I had often wandered why I felt these strong emotions and had felt strange having them. They were a bit unnatural. I felt relieved that it was an illness that was making me act like this, and that it wasn't solely my personality. I was assured that with medication and therapy it too would be resolved. I felt my friends had reached breaking point and were lost at how to cope with me, so contact more or less stopped. Around the same time, I successfully auditioned for a competitive dance crew. It became the one thing I was passionate about: that and my new puppy Louis, mum bought me him to give me a focus, someone to look after and my newest hobby, smoking my lungs away. The girls in this new circle became my new support. It was all new to them, so initially they showed me the compassion I was searching for. Soon though, my illness drove them away too. They shared the same helplessness that my old friends had felt.

As my week in the ward drew to a close I did not feel confident that I was ready to leave. I lived in fear the binges would return and I still needed the support of the staff. My consultant ignored my opinions. I think he was scared because of the BPD, that I would grow more and more emotionally involved and become more needy than independent.

"Why am I being punished...does everyone think I'm lying about how bad things are...I'm going to die if this continues"

So I was back home; angry and fearful. And all too soon my worst fears came true. The second day I was home the bingeing restarted. I do not remember what I ate – A little? A lot? But it felt worthy of cutting my arm ... badly. Blood poured out but I did not care. I bandaged it up myself and went to bed. I did not care if I bled to death. I had lost all hope.

"I'm so unhappy, distressed and inconsolable...I'm a fat f*cking failure...I wish I could starve to death, but I'm too obsessed with food"

The next day I met with Susan. She was shocked by my emotional state and horrified at the mess of my still, bleeding arm. She took me straight back to the ward I had just left. The staff were amazing. My self-harm had been a cry for help and it had worked. It was a really negative reinforcement for someone vulnerable like me, but sadly it's what I wanted.

I was to stay in the ward now, and I felt relieved. But the next three weeks did not go well like the first one had. I was restricting but finding it increasingly difficult. I was bingeing on anything I could get my hands on, through lying or stealing. I felt powerless to it and could not stop. I felt disgusted at my behaviour so started burning myself as I had no access to **sharp** objects. Burning led to me getting infections, continuously in my arms.

"not usually am I lost for words, but I feel speechless with despair...I know I always say I want to die, but I literally believe it now...I'm gonna starve to death"

My body
I hate you so much. My skin crawls at the very thought of you. You disgust and repulse me, and I know it's my own entire fault. I cannot bare to look at you. I cover you in layers of clothes, baggy and unrevealing. My pen scars the

paper as I have scarred you. I've taken glass, razors and blades to your once childlike arms, as I cannot cope with how you look. You are meant to depict how I feel. When you look frail and weak I can once again be that ill girl; the person people will look at and envy or see the pain, the power of her mind. I want the ability back to starve you until I can't walk, I've dreamed of it since the age of ten. The media flaunted these skinny girls, bodies laced with bones and everyone at home dieted around me. I did the same. With no other options, no other thoughts, I told myself; I just want to be thin. But no number was low enough. No weight heals a screaming mind. When you're frail you're close death but surrounded by love. Now I'm engulfed in this hell and I don't just mean my mind. What I really mean is this fat and hideous body, I hate this body. I fear you will never shift and just keep growing; I'll be obese before I know it. I'm literally scared of my own body. My mind is out of control; it tells me to eat and eat, get thinner and thinner. I fear going to bed, to wake up to this nightmare.

I would speak to my 'chosen' members of staff. The BPD made me have a horrible jealousy of other patients who took up their time. I felt rejected and hurt if they weren't constantly with me. It was like an obsession that grew the more time I was with them, and even more when I was alone.

"Why is she talking to Katie? I want to speak to her; I need to speak to her. She understands. Without her I'll be alone with my thoughts and that is unthinkable"

About two and a half weeks into my stay I felt unbearably

low and could envision no way forward, no way out. I spilled the same ramble of thoughts to the same nurses numerous times a day. I wanted to be thin, my anorexic past may have been hell, but this was so much worse. The bingeing was becoming more regular and staff's time was more occupied by unruly patients. I had once again had enough. I saw no way out so took the 3rd overdose of the year; I am ashamed even to write it. The last thing I remember was apologising to the nurses, especially the one who had been so supportive to me. I had stored the medication in my hospital drawer. I felt safe in the knowledge I could take it if things became too much. I did not think I would overdose, but again I seemed not to be the one in control. I was admitted to Accident and Emergency and spend days in a hazed, spaced out state.

Again it was decided that I was to leave the ward as being there was clearly not benefiting me. I was angry at my consultant for making me go home the first time, when I said I was not ready to, and now my anger returned ... I was a million times worse off. I was angry that no-one could help me. I was angry that I was seen to be the only one who could control the situation - I couldn't. He said that I was slipping into the 'patient' role, and becoming less independent, much to the frustration of the staff (and I suppose myself).

But home was to show no improvement. The bingeing was ruling my life. I wore baggy tracksuits all the time instead of my regular clothes. Generally because my clothes did not fit but also, I did not want anyone to see how fat I had got. My weight was the highest it had ever been and I was in a deep depression, self-harming daily, and therefore visiting A and E just as often. Self-harm served as a means of punishment. I was tortured by my out of control, manic eating. I wanted to feel the pain of a blade on my skin, the burning of my flesh. I wanted to SHOW myself that I had done wrong.

Mum kept my wallet to deter me from buying food. Embarrassingly to me, she also resorted to locking food away in the garage. Decent attempts, but I always found a way around it. I would raid the house for money and even steal from the shops. I could not rid my mind of this impulse/desire to eat and eat and never stop. But at the same time my mind was all consumed with anorexia. I dreamed and idolised the way I used to be. I wanted to, or felt I needed to be that girl again.

Have you ever hated someone or something so much that you'd give up anything, do anything just to make it go away? Would you scar your own body, lie to the people you love, just in the hope that you can return to the one thing that ever gave you happiness? I would. I do. I'm not in control. I never have I been. I've been bullied and tortured, beaten and abused by a voice I've been forced to share my life with. I had a power, a strength that others didn't. Shivering and weak yet protected and admired. I love her. So why did I lose her? I need to find her. She cannot die because if she does then I will too. I think about her every second of every day. I want her now. I will then be the person that people can love. I will be happy. Her voice I felt blessed with, but now I hear the devil. What did I do so wrong to deserve this parasite within me? It crept in slowly, secretly, but it's now a beast who rules my life, making me eat unthinkable amounts, then throw up from the physical inability to hold it within me. It puts me in a trance-like state where I feel numb, then I come to, and the terror rains over me. Death is all it can bring as a life with it, I refuse to live.

My eating disorder had changed and it seemed to be going in the opposite direction from what my head wanted. From what I wanted. Every night I would pray that I could starve the next day and shrink back to my old skinny self, but each day I only seemed to eat more than I did the previous. Hell would be an understatement. As my past life seemed so far from reach, rather than idealising a healthy life, I wanted back every security anorexia brought me. I had people trying to help me: a dietician who tried to adapt a menu plan to get me 'back on track', and a consultant constantly changing my many tablets, but nothing was working. It was this that led to the most horrific overdose that I would ever experience. I would never want to go through that again. I thought the pain killers would instantly kill me. That's what I wanted. I wanted an end to this terrifying existence. Instead it led to the worst twenty-four hours of my life.

I lay down to sleep, believing I would never wake again. I wrote letters of regret to my loved ones. I felt pain at leaving them but little panic within myself. It wasn't until I woke two hours later struggling to breathe, that my emotions erupted. I was rushed to A and E, and violently sick for twelve long hours. My stomach muscles were in so much pain, I hallucinated every time I closed my eyes that there was a man in the corner of the room with a gun, and I experienced extreme panic attacks and headaches. Although I had taken the tablets to kill myself, I became petrified at the thought of dying. I believed that if I closed my eyes I would be gone, and no amount of re-assurance could convince me otherwise. It was hell; there are no other words for it.

The staff at the hospital sat and comforted me, I was terrified and felt so guilty that this was all self inflicted. My liver was damaged and they were pumping special drugs into a drip in my arm. I just had to be patient. They said if I hadn't woken with the panic attack when I did, I would have had possible liver failure and died. After twenty-four hours I started to feel brighter. I was shocked at what I had just put myself, my family, and Craig through. The thought of swallowing another tablet was enough to make me sick. I vowed to everyone that I would never overdose again. Dying became so much more serious than I had let myself believe. The pain was not worth it. I had to move on. I was discharged on the Saturday, feeling as though I had the world's worst hangover. But by the Saturday night I was feeling really ill again. My head thumped and as I tried to sleep I sweated through six pairs of pyjamas. By the morning I was weak. Mum called the hospital and they told me to come back in. I was checked and it turned out that some of the burns on my arm had got badly infected. Again I experienced torture. I cried constantly, was in severe pain, and shot from hot to cold. I made a second promise – to never self-harm again. I had, again, scared myself, and never wanted to feel like that.

As with everything else about my illness I soon forgot (or blocked out) how bad it had been. I refrained from bingeing, but as soon as it returned I was back to cutting and unfortunately another overdose. I can see the pain I caused everyone who cared about me. The pain I put my mum through horrifies me. She no longer sleeps, in fear of what I might be doing on my 'bad' days, behind my closed door. My illness takes its toll on me but is having just as big an impact on her. I worry. I am scared that like me she cannot cope anymore, that she will snap under the pressure, and that it will all be my fault. I love her so much and wish I could stop the hurt she feels. I know others probably blame me, but let me tell them that I most definitely would not be this way if I had a choice.

"Mum is in bits. She says that she can't cope with me anymore ... What do I do? ... She says if I die it would be a million times worse .... Am I selfish to want to die?"
Craig too felt the strain of my illness as I pushed him away or cried uncontrollably in his arms. He described himself as being more of a carer than a boyfriend. My illness was spreading like wildfire.

My eating disorder definitely does not just affect me but everyone who is close by. At times I feel my friends have given up on me, but I know that they just find it so hard to see, or wait for me to keep on slipping back ... for me to start "destroying myself again" as one of my friends put it. My sister often says when I am so ill and low that she is losing a sister, and her daughters, their auntie. I guess these things can serve a purpose to only motivate me into a full recovery.

Help at hand

With the self-harm and suicide attempts ever increasing my consultant arranged for me to see a self-harm support worker. Slowly we would chip away at my eating disorder, as this is inevitably what led to the self-harm and suicide attempts. Soon she felt helpless in my world and like so many others: abandoned me.

So day by day my manic world seemed to be spiralling more and more out of control. I constantly thought and dreamed about dying. I felt it was my only way out. I didn't want to hurt those who loved me but I needed out. I imagined taking pills and jumping from a bridge, hanging myself, or crashing my car into a brick wall. It was extreme.

Is it raining outside, 'cause there's thunder in my head? Death and destruction is all I can think about. I'm alone and at one of the lowest points. I do not want to be seen, I do not want to wake tomorrow. I want to lay to rest forever. I know I'm never going to achieve what I want, and without her I cannot go on. Existing in this grotesque body is too much for me, and the bingeing devil will just not leave. I can't do this. I can feel eyes upon me, thinking I'm fine cause I don't weight five stone, thinking life must eventually be treating me well as I don't have a tube

hanging from my nose. Well look at my arms, this is my
pain, this is how I'm telling you how bad things are.
If I had a wish, I'd wish to be thin, frail and have more
strength than I have now. I'm a fat girl with an anorexic
mind. I'm told I feel so little about myself that I cannot
cope with a life of just being me. I need to have this
mask: this shield that protects me from myself, that was
anorexia!
I may still be alive but I'm dead inside. No-one can help
but please someone save me!

I was finding my everyday existence too much to tolerate, as was my mum. The binges were extreme and I was becoming too low to fight them. I felt as though I was doomed for a life where my body was growing as fast as my looming thoughts. My consultant was strongly against me going into an acute psychiatric ward as all previous admissions had ended in the same way – in disaster. We both knew that these environments were not specialised to deal with my intense illness, and so a respite association was found for me.

It was situated near my family home and was an ideal break for everyone involved. I was to go for a week at a time, stay at the house, and receive support from the staff there. The relief at handing over responsibility was indescribable. I had my own room, and with there always being at least three staff on shift at any one time, I was able to openly talk about my distress. I could offload without fearing I was burdening them, like I felt I did with my mum. Over the space of three months I went to the respite centre about every second week. It was more than was planned but it was what I needed.

As with everything regarding me, the good feelings, the

benefits did not last. It was on my last visit to the respite home that my compulsive eating spiralled of control. I used my stay purely to feed my addiction: food. I would eat copious amounts of cereal, and toast smeared in butter. I would raid the cook's cupboards for anything to silence my mind from the screaming desire to eat. I shudder at the thought of how extreme things had become. I was literally crawling from my room to the kitchen, eating, throwing up, and then sleeping in a haze of sugared emotion. This lasted a couple of days and I felt horrific. I cut my arms, had to have seventeen staples to heal the gaping wounds, then made the decision to leave the respite house and never return. It felt like yet another lifeline had been cut from my existence.

A plan

My social worker and my consultant were growing increasingly concerned at the horrific chaos that was becoming my life. My mum too was feeling the trauma of my illness. She has always been so involved in my life, but with anorexia there, she had no control over helping me. It is exhausting her like nothing else on earth. She cried through sleepless nights. Tears I wish I did not have to have heard. All she wanted, I know, was what was best for me, and for me to be happy. I looked at my nieces and imagined how I would feel if they were doing the things I was doing to myself. The thought was unbearable. It was clear to us all that living at home was not going to keep me safe, so it was decided that I should be put forward for a flat in supported accommodation.

Supported accommodation is a set up whereby you have your own flat and independence, but have trained professionals available for support twenty-four hours a day, in their own flat nearby. I was keen for the move but mum was apprehensive. I knew I couldn't go on the way things were and was willing to try absolutely anything. The process was rather quick: Susan applied with an application form that I'm told is not dissimilar to this book - it explained me inside out. I think this in depth account allowed the team at the supported accommodation to evaluate exactly how they could help me and I am so thankful for her efforts.

Not long after, I was assigned a flat. The excitement was incredible. My own place. A fresh start. A new me. A life free of my problems of the past. I would have people there all the time, stopping me from bingeing, and allowing me to openly talk through the inner distresses I was experiencing. I went in with an open mind and heart. I felt this was the key. My expectations and hopes were higher than ever.

Decorating, what can only be described as a shell of a place, was extremely pleasurable. I was definitely putting my own stamp on my new home. The artist within me seeped through. It took about three weeks to complete and I think I only binged two or three times. I had such a focus in my life that there was no time for this disruptive behaviour to haunt me. But sure enough if the slightest of things went wrong – whether it be that I chose the wrong colour paint, or discovered a leaky radiator, I took my distress out on food, and thereafter, further punished myself by any means possible. One particular night I felt desperation like no other. Mum was guarding me from my agonising thoughts but the need to reprimand myself for committing my sin, of binging, was too strong. I went upstairs and poured bleach into my mouth. I did not swallow. My intentions were 'only' to burn my taste buds in the hope I would no longer need or desire food. The bleach ripped through my mouth and into my throat. As I spat it out I could still feel its presence: it lingered for days. Mum and dad were both horrified by my actions. Mum says she will never get her head around what I did to myself. In the days following I found it hard to eat. The essence of bleach was embedded in my mouth, but my plan did not last. Not long after, food became the ruler in my hopeless existence, once again.

Time came to move into my new dwelling. I was excited and nervous all at once. I met the staff one by one, and with each introduction I bonded and became more confident in my decision that this was the right move. This was going to work!

"The staff at my flat are incredible. They will be my saviours"

It was agreed that four or five times a day, they would spend time with me. They were in control of my medication and money. It was the perfect set up. I wanted no room for slip ups. I wanted it to be the perfect transition to the start of my new life. I embraced the freedom along with their support, and felt a sense of pride and satisfaction if I got through yet another day without bingeing.

I m falling

My optimism was maybe too grand? It is true what they say: that you can move anywhere but your problems will always follow you. Craig left for a work trip to Egypt for four weeks, and I was left without my rock. This was not what led to what seems like a very quick deterioration, but without his support, and love, I felt lost.

The connection I felt to the staff was ever growing. They were my new support network and were making every effort possible to understand and manage my disorder, but I was growing ever more deceitful as the urges to binge manifested through my inability to lead what I deemed, a stable life. I would keep money and raid my flat of any food items. I'd spend small or large amounts on packets of biscuits, chocolate, sweets, and ice-cream. I was unable to eat as much as I had in the past: be it fear or my stomach had just had enough, but I was bingeing, then throwing up or using laxatives to further punish my body. Any ability I had to cope with the feelings afterwards, or to even rationalise what I had eaten, had disappeared. I was mortified at my actions, and punishment was the only way I could envision a way out. Clearly it never worker.

"Why, why, why? I'm so angry I could destroy this flat, me, everything…who cursed me with this life…I hate anorexia for leaving and bringing me this beast!"

After, I would always think: "If only I had gone to staff first...". It's an easy thing to say in hindsight, but when an addiction is so strong it compels you to do the one thing that inevitably will destroy you.

Within the space of fourteen days I had visited Accident and Emergency seven times. The receptionists knew what to type into her computer, as soon as I walked through the door screen. I took an overdose, drenched my mouth in bleach, severely cut and burnt my arms. To say I was a mess was an understatement, and concern was growing from every angle.

The staff at my flat I believe were truly terrified, and my consultant and social worker were doing anything possible to relieve the situation. Things just were not improving; in fact they were getting considerably worse. My new found freedom had sent me into a universe of bingeing and guilt free self mutilation.

As friends and family expressed their need for me to be hospitalised, I felt anger towards my consultant for not being willing to admit me to the psychiatric ward. His reasoning was valid; each time I had been in there before, there had been no evidence of any improvement. But I took his lack of action as a disregard to my emotional state. I was finding living alone unbearable, even with the intense support I was receiving. I told my mum nothing of what was going on in fear of further burdening her, therefore sought comfort in my eldest sister Laura. Laura has a detached nature; in the nicest possible way! She cares no end for me and my family's well being, and has been a rock to me throughout my illness. She too suffered from anorexia as a child. I remember nothing of this as I was a toddler at the time. Even she struggles to recall details of her illness, but her experience has given her a greater understanding and respect for my problems. Unlike Karen, Laura is able to emotionally detach herself from the situation. Rather than getting upset, she offers reassurance and, I suppose, a levelled headed opinion. She doesn't preach or get angry, she holds it together in times of crisis, but by no means gives into my eating disordered mind or behaviours. Family are often too close to talk to, friends I feel, I do not want to strain, and professionals often have 'too clinical' an opinion; Laura gave me what I needed.

Laura expressed her concern, and the possibility that I was heading in the direction of hospital. It was on one meeting with my consultant that I broke down in despair. I pleaded that I couldn't go on like I was, and that I was losing the will to live. I was fighting a losing battle. It was then he mentioned the new eating disorder in-patient unit in the city. My head screamed no. The thoughts of past experiences' of emaciated girls, with tubes hanging from their noses, plagued my mind. I was heavier than ever and couldn't bare the thought of exposing myself to that anorexic world. He reassured me that my worst fears would not be brought to light, but I felt doubtful. However the mere fact that I was even considering this option showed me how horrific things had got. Every time I had been admitted before my weight had been dangerously low and I would demand that I was too fat to go in; this time was very different. I was at a 'healthy' weight, and so the plan would only be to maintain this. The real reason for this admission was to get me the intense support that I so very clearly needed. I was only overweight in my eyes. Because my weight was higher than when I left the last eating disorder unit, I felt it was wrong for me to be returning to another. I believed I was a disgrace. A fraud. I worried that everyone else there, would think this too.

The decision came as a shock to me and even more so, to mum. She hated the thought of me once again being in a unit where eating disorders were our only one thing in common.

My consultant allowed me home on the provision that I would meet with Susan in the afternoon. As I left his office he called the unit to see if they agreed that I would benefit from such an intense programme. I met with her, but not before I binged and self harmed. I was mentally bruised, emotionally drained, and physically exhausted. I cried tears of hopelessness and despair. I wanted her to hold me like the child who was screaming inside to be helped. I wanted her to reassure me that everything was going to be okay. I was suicidal and more than anything wanted an end to this madness. She spoke in depth to my consultant as I anxiously sat in the waiting room. On return she confirmed his earlier decision: that the unit would be the best place for me. They gave me no time to think, no time to prepare. I would receive a call in the morning with their final decision. I had a restless evening: replaying memories of past hospital admissions, restricting food in the anticipation of going in, making endless lists of reasons why I should or should not enter a place that would inevitable make or break me.

Eden

The next day was a haze. Before I knew what I was really doing, I was standing, terrified, in a room in the new unit. I felt almost as though I wasn't really there. I was experiencing it, but most definitely not living it. I was not there to fight against them like I had in previous admissions. This time I wanted helped more than anything. Although this was the case, it did not stop the terror within.

Mum came with me and showed more emotion than I did. She heard the tails unravel of my most recent harming; the deterioration I rather her not know. I believe she was thinking "Here we go again … back in hospital, back to square one, back to the emotional, distressed, inconsolable little girl". But, I was to prove everyone wrong. The unit wasn't laced with emaciated girls, and the atmosphere was generally very positive and reassuring. I knew some of the girls from previous hospital admissions, but it was clear I was a different person from the one they once knew. I wasn't crying, weak, and scared; I was positive, determined and motivated. I just needed a kick in the right direction.

I instantly bonded with the staff. It had been two years since I had been in such an intense, specialised setting. They were trained with the knowledge and guidance I needed.

I saw the dietician, not as an enemy, but as someone who was going to enable me to destroy my harmful relationship with food, and build a much healthier one. My key worker, Lindsey, showed me the life I could lead, she never held back with her opinions and soon told me when my thoughts were clearly not Vicky's. Her insight reminded me greatly of Emma's, and her 'no-nonsense' attitude worked well with me. There was an amazing Occupational Therapist there too, who could channel my thoughts in a direction I did not think possible. To my surprise and delight, Angie, my old support worker, started working in the unit. It was like my lifelines were all returned to me, and getting stronger by the second.

In the first couple of weeks the urges to binge remained, but I was kept safe, through not being allowed out alone and having a menu plan that satisfied my hunger. At home, when I wasn't bingeing, I was starving myself. Though the binges were generally spurred on by emotional situations, the fact I was depriving my body of what it needed; inevitably I set myself up for a fall.

This unit was different from anywhere I had previously been. We were all treated as individuals and not just 'another anorexic or bulimic'. My care was tailored to meet MY needs and I was given time to unscramble my messed up head, my illness! I lost some of the weight I had gained because my body was settling itself and thanking me for treating it healthily again, and I began to actually accept my body. Gone were the tracksuits I had worn for the last year ... Hello Topshop! Soon even the urges to binge began to fade. I went forty-four days without a single blip. To me this was more progress than I ever believed possible. It allowed my eyes and mind to open to a life free of an eating disorder.

I witnessed patients in the early stages who resembled me in the other unit. I felt no jealousy towards their situation or skeletal frames. I felt pity. I knew anorexia was never going to solve my problems; she would only simply embark on a path to create them.

With willingness I actually wanted to get better. I believe I had hit rock bottom. I realised that I needed a new means of survival. The binges returned but in the mildest form, and rarely. I discovered that punishing myself through self-harm would not un-do what I had eaten, or affect my weight, and I was being taught to pick myself up from a blip, and move on with the day. It was crucial advise.

In the unit I cried, I laughed, I struggled, but most importantly, I improved. At the last meeting with everyone involved in my care, whilst an inpatient, my consultant praised me for not turning into a 'patient', into my usual 'sick' roll. He praised me for coming into the unit with my head held high, to search for Vicky, and to kick the crap out of my eating disorder.

I was discharged after two months. I can honestly say I felt happy. Unfortunately I still strive for perfection and want everyday to be amazing, but slowly I am learning to take the highs with the lows. I attended the unit five days a week as an outpatient, to ensure I was still on track, mentally and physically and the rest of the time was mine. It all became a bit much in the end and I left to be with an outpatient team. I needed out of the 'eating disordered community'.

The staff at my accommodation have been invaluable. They spend endless hours with me: talking, encouraging, and introducing me to a better life. I started seeing my friends again, they have thankfully welcomed me back with open arms. My weekends are all about shopping.

I also got accepted to study Fashion Management at University, starting later this year. Things are looking up.

Craig and I ended our relationship, thankfully on good terms. My thoughts about my sexuality are no longer secret, and everyone accepts me, proving that my worst fears were clearly irrational. It makes me wander that maybe, if I hadn't been so disapproving of myself and my feelings two years ago, I would have continued on in my previous spell of progress. I guess now I am in a better, more mature and understanding place in my mind, that there is no benefit in my 'what ifs'.

I feel less apprehensive about the future and what it holds. I do not always feel alone and if I slip I know there are many safety nets waiting to catch me. I count myself extremely lucky. I know I couldn't have come this far, and I can't continue to succeed alone. But I am not alone. I am so relieved that we have eventually found a system that works for me. Throughout my illness my family have expressed distress, at times when there was little support available, when I was not in hospital. We were searching for something like we have now, but it has taken years to get it. I worry for other sufferers looking for help and hope reading this, I offer some sort of help.

I am more prepared for what life throws at me, and guess that life is never worth giving up on: tomorrow is ALWAYS a new day! I now have hopes and dreams for the future. No longer is it bleak and out of reach. There is light at the end of my tunnel.

My picture is by no means perfect. I have days where I feel like I am back at square one and where picking myself up seems all too hard to do; days when I have urges and desires to follow my eating disordered past. I wander then if I'll ever truly recover and be free, if I can completely rid my mind of the demons of my past once and for all, but I know I'm in a much better place to try, and I guess only time will tell. My eating disorder has lasted 11 long years and simply putting two fingers up to it isn't enough to undo its damage, but I have the tools if I am willing to fight. I still binge, restrict and self harm at times, I just hope I feel the contentment soon to put some of this to rest. My self-esteem and confidence have been cruelly diminished over the years and I know this is the area where work really needs done. I want to embrace being an individual, not feeling like I have to be like everyone else or 'normal': 'unique' I'd like to be able to call myself. Anorexia brought me this uniqueness, made me feel special, cared for and like a child, but I am almost twenty-four now so I need to find my adult self.

I feel relieved that my nieces are both young enough to have ignored the horrors of my past and hope I can give them the brightest of futures. I know the signs all too well, and would never want them or anyone else to have to experience the things I have.

It has taken a very long time to get to where I am today. Some might say too long, but I believe you have to be truly ready, willing and equipped in order to recover successfully. Through my eating disorder I have experienced too many bad times and hand on heart, know I should never return there. I will slip along the way, but maybe there is enough people to catch me now if I fall. Wounded I have been and wounded I still am...I just need time to heal.

About the Author

Vicky writes a true an inspiring account of the true hell she has experienced: from what started as anorexia nervosa and spread into a multitude of crippling mental health problems. she speaks from the heart and does not hold on back on informing the reader of the truth behind, what is so often seen, as a self inflicted illness.

Lightning Source UK Ltd.
Milton Keynes UK
25 June 2010

156100UK00001B/12/P